Quickbooks

Expert With Useful Tips & Tricks to Master the Quickbooks

(Learn How to Get Over Bookkeeping and Accounting in a Very Simple)

Richard McNeil

Published By **Elena Holly**

Richard McNeil

All Rights Reserved

Quickbooks: Expert With Useful Tips & Tricks to Master the Quickbooks (Learn How to Get Over Bookkeeping and Accounting in a Very Simple)

ISBN 978-1-77485-998-8

No part of this guidebook shall be reproduced in any form without permission in writing from the publisher except in the case of brief quotations embodied in critical articles or reviews.

Legal & Disclaimer

from and against any damages, costs, and expenses, including any legal fees potentially resulting from the application of any of the information provided by this guide. This disclaimer applies to any damages or injury caused by the use and application, whether directly or indirectly, of any advice or information presented, whether for breach of contract, tort, negligence, personal injury, criminal intent, or under any other cause of action.

You agree to accept all risks of using the information presented inside this book. You need to consult a professional medical practitioner in order to ensure you are both able and healthy enough to participate in this program.

Table Of Contents

Chapter 1: Configuring Quickbooks

QuickBooks Online is easy to install and begin using. It's so easy that it is possible to have your business file set up within less than 20 minutes. There are a few important actions to follow to be sure that you're setting up your business files effectively and with precision.

The setup has been optimized for speed and ease of use but it requires some training. This chapter will focus on making sure you have the QuickBooks business account set up and operating.

By the time you've reached the end of this chapter by the end of this chapter, you should have the ability to:

* Create a company file

* Configure the basics of settings

* Create basic accounts

* Import list details for the company File Setup

There are many ways to setup your company's file. Making sure it is set up correctly will assist you as well as your Bookkeeper or Accountant keep up to date in regards to GST and payroll tax. To use QuickBooks Online, your business or you have to sign up for the software. The business can join through intuit.com and registering to get a free trial. Your accountant can create the business file using Accounting Online QuickBooks.

Company File Creation

First of all, you have to make a business file. It's the place you keep the financial records of your business. You can begin from scratch by creating a brand new business file or import and convert data from another small-business program. For those who don't have any experience with bookkeeping there's always the option to use an existing file that someone else has created. For example, if you've received assistance from an accountant in the beginning of your business They may be in a position to assist you once more by providing you with a QuickBooks business file that's specifically tailored to your business and help you get a headstart.

If you don't have an accountant don't worry, we'll help you through the process of setting everything up to ensure that you never require one. It's a good thing that QuickBooks is a breeze to use and creating a business account isn't rocket science.

In the first section, we will show you how to get started with QuickBooks. If you're beginning your company's new file We will walk to you via your QuickBooks setting dialog along with an Easy Step Interview to get you up and running (and to determine which chapters will assist you in getting your task completed). However when you're switching from another software and want to make the process as smooth as possible. We will also go through opening the company file as well as making it up to date with the most recent version of QuickBooks as well as basic modifications to company information.

* Start with visiting the QuickBooks site https://quickbooks.intuit.com, then signing in with your QuickBooks Online account. When the website is open choose the "Create New Company" option, which is located under the "File" menu in the toolbar.

Select"Start Interview "Start interview" option and start answering those questions.

Please enter your company's information It isn't necessary to enter anything other than the company's name, but in the interest of saving time and making it easier later on, you must complete all required details.

* Selecting your industry of business is the next step. When you select the type of your business, QuickBooks will customize its settings to meet the demands of your company.

Select the kind of business you want to run (sole proprietorship or partnership, corporation and more.). A correct choice of your company organizational type will also facilitate tax preparation later on.

* Select the month which is the first of the annual accounting cycle. The month of January is typically the beginning month for the accounting period that is annual, however this is able to be altered according to the company's preferences.

Create the administrator's password. This is crucial when no other person other than yourself has access access to the computer, or company file. Only you car access the entire QuickBooks firm file. Choose "Next" and then select where you would like the company's data to be saved

The Customization of QuickBooks for Your Business

It is the QuickBooks Home page is laid out similarly to the procedure that you use when you're doing accounting, which is why it functions as a map for various accounting tasks you'll need to complete. Other shortcuts to QuickBooks features are sprinkled across the left icon bar, top icon bar as well as Vendor Customers, Employees, and Vendor Centers. Your business isn't the same as any other. If you're running an entirely cash-sales company and you don't have any concern about invoices or customer lists and deposits, even though it is a regular occurrence. However, you don't need to agree with QuickBooks as the first version of the ease of use. The Home page as well as the icon bars have the most frequently used shortcuts. However, you can also add, delete or rearrange and modify the features that appear on there. Additionally, you can add preferred windows, features and report options to your Favorites menu. This chapter will cover all of your choices.

Alongside tweaking QuickBooks its layout it also lets you customize the form templates that the program offers. QuickBooks can help you get up and running using built-in templates for business forms. These templates are great if you need to send out invoices. However, if you do manage to get a few time, you can design templates that display the data you're looking for, formatted in according to your preferences and laid out in accordance using your letterhead. You can make as many copies as you like. For instance, you could create an invoice template to create a letterhead print, and another one for electronic invoices to email addresses that include your logo, your company's name as well as your address.

This chapter outlines the most effective methods to design forms (using QuickBooks Form designs or templates built into QuickBooks as a base for creating your own.) Further on in this book you'll learn how you can improve the quality of forms using advanced techniques for customization and build templates by hand.

* Continue to complete questions from the Easy Step Interview Questions to create custom Quickbooks for your business.

If your company is solely in selling products choose "Products solely". If you offer services along with the sale of products "Both items and the services" is the best option.

* Indicate if you sell products and/or services on the internet.

* Choose whether you will charge sales tax.

* If you are providing custom-designed work or any other service that QuickBooks to prepare estimates, choose "Yes".

* If you are a vendor and take orders from customers and would like Quickbooks to keep track of the orders, choose "Yes".

* If you would like to use receipts for sales Select "Yes".

* If you'd like to to create and send invoices, click "Yes".

* If you wish to use partial billing to make payment, click "Yes" to utilize the process of invoicing.

* Click "Yes" If you would like to track due bills and receive reminders of the date they're due.

• If you are printing checks, or accept credit cards, you must select the correct answer.

* Choose the response you prefer for tracking inventory.

* Choose "Yes" when your business includes more workers. If you want to track the time spent on projects completed by your staff or by you choose "Yes".

* If your company is involved in several currencies, choose the correct response.

Accounting in QuickBooks: To establish your accounts, you will need to be aware of the date you'd like to begin from and also how you'd prefer to manage your earnings and expenses.

Then, pick the date you will begin to cover your financial obligations. An important reminder that, no matter what date you pick, all commercial activity that been conducted since that date has to be recorded. Therefore, it's easier and more efficient to select an earlier date when you begin monitoring your finances in QuickBooks.

* Enter the correct bank account details, including the last statement from the bank that ended date and balance

QuickBooks suggests a collection of accounts for expenses and income in accordance with the selection of industry you made during the interview. But, you are able to examine these account choices and then select or remove accounts that better reflect your company's needs. Changes or additions to your chart of accounts or to any or part of your Easy Step Interview can be anytime after the establishment of your company's file.

Affamiliarizing yourself With the QuickBooks Homepage

Since you've had more than enough tasks to handle the day-to-day running of your business, you don't want your bookkeeping to take longer than is necessary. QuickBooks The left icon bar and the top icon bar provide shortcuts to your preferred features. Each icon bar comes with its pros and cons so you have to choose which you prefer (or you can switch off all icons completely). This chapter explains how to use QuickBooks features via the menu bar or icons. In a lively bookkeeping session, you may be able to have multiple QuickBooks window open at the same time. This chapter will help you will learn how to manage all windows that you are opening. If you prefer to concentrate on a single task it is possible to tell QuickBooks to only display the one windows at a.

Like its name suggests, Supermax view expands windows to let you get more information without scrolling. There are a lot of window techniques in this section. Another method to complete your accounting efficiently and quickly is by using features accessible via your QuickBooks Home page. The page is not just a an overview of the bookkeeping chores you carry out often, but it also provides you with fast access to tasks as well as information about vendors employees, customers, and customers as well as the functions and financial data you need frequently. Select an icon and the appropriate window or dialog box will open that includes charts of Accounts, Item List Writing Checks, or, of course, everyone's favorite -- Make deposits. This chapter explains how you can utilize the workflow icons that appear that appear on your Home Page along with the Customer, Vendor and Employees Centers which open when you click on the appropriate buttons on the panels on the Home page. Additionally, you ll learn how to look over your company's financials using the window for Company Snapshot.

The QuickBooks homepage is split into several sections which are well-organized and linked by workflow arrows to assist you in managing and completing your business tasks more efficiently, quicker and more efficiently.

Vendors: The Vendor area in the workflow diagram as well as the center for vendors accessible via the toolbar will help you keep track of the purchases you make from various vendors and also categorizing your expenses. You can make and modify your vendor list and purchase orders and also enter and pay invoices for your company. The vendor center provides you with a an entire view of where your cash is going. On one screen, can view the entire list of your vendors, and precisely the amount you have to pay them. Click on the name of a vendor to access their complete history of the vendor. There is no need to create separate reports to determine the exact amount of business you're conducting with each vendor. You can also sort your bills according to due date to ensure you're always on top of your financials. If you have to speak to the vendor, just click the name of the vendor to view the contact details. If a vendor contacts you to inquire about an unpaid bill and you want to look up the invoice quickly and view the check's number and the date you made the payment.

Customers The Customer area and center will assist you manage all sales made to customers. It allows you to prepare estimate and invoices. It also lets you keep track of accounts and generate statements, in addition to accepting the payment and creating receipts for sales. The customers ' center serves as an overview of all your customer data. Instead of having to sort through many screens, you will be able to view the list of all your customers and get the relevant information for each one of them. Click on the name of a client and immediately you can will see the entire interaction you've had with them. You can also see the contact details (phone number or fax number) as well as the terms of payment)

Employees: Notifying the Easy Step Interview that you employ employees will result in employees centers to be established in order to improve and control your staff. The employee center allows you to know exactly what you're making each worker. Click on the name of an employee to see their payroll record. If you're looking to get to the worker, the contact info is in front of you.

The Company section of the diagram of workflow will allow users to control lists that include the chart of accounts, as well as service and item lists.

Banking: Banking section allows you to keep track of all deposits, as well as print and sign checks to any of the bank accounts you have.

The icons that appear on the homepage depend on your answers during your Easy Step Interview. If you answered that you'd like to make an estimate using QuickBooks the "Estimates" icon is likely to be displayed in the Customers section in the event that it is not, however there is no "Estimates" icon won't be displayed. If you'd like to modify any of the settings made during the Easy Step Interview, select Edit Preferences from the toolbar. You can alter the preferences of your company or personal preferences at any time.

Set up of Customers, Vendors and jobs

Perhaps you like strutting around your sales team shouting "We aren't achieving anything until somebody has sold something! "It is possible to repeat the same maxim within your accounting department, too.

It doesn't matter if you offer products or services, making your first sale by introducing the new customer can lead to many possible actions that could be taken, such as but not just making the entry of a new customer and establishing a task to do the work, and finally the highly anticipated and desired goal of invoicing (delivering an invoice for the service or the goods purchased that outlines the amount the buyer owes) your client with the purpose of collecting revenue. The people to whom you offer services or products are known by a variety of names, including customers, shoppers, consumers members, consumers, etc. The QuickBooks dictionary, there's just one term that is appropriate for the individual, group (or group) of individuals that purchase items and services you offer and that word is customer. In QuickBooks customers, they are the documentation of data about your live customer. QuickBooks uses the data you have entered on your customers. Using this information, it, you can create sales forms, as well as invoices that contain your customer's name as well as payment terms, address and any other details.

Customers from the real world are crucial to success, but do the customers you have in QuickBooks actually important? Even if you run a suppose, for instance, a cash-based primary business, storing your customers' information in Quickbooks isn't an awful idea. For example the creation of QuickBooks records for your recurring customers of your store can cut the time needed to enter their details with each new purchase through the use of an automated system. If your business is project-oriented, you could assign a task for every project you initiate for a client in QuickBooks. In QuickBooks the definition of the term "project" refers to each task that you agreed (or was requested to sign) to complete to a customer, whether it's fixing a yacht or putting up a billboard advertisement and so on. Let's suppose you're an electrician and work for general contractors regularly.

You could set up a variety of tasks, such as one for setting up Jobs, Customers, and Vendors for each of the places you work: Scott estate, Hammond estate as well as Julliard estate. It is then possible to view the income and expenses by job , and analyze the efficiency of each of them. If your company does not handle work, there's no need to create them in QuickBooks. Record stores, for instance, sell records, not services or projects. If your company isn't performing tasks, you could add customers to QuickBooks and then maintain invoices, or perhaps creating sales receipts for purchases. But, before you can begin receiving payments, you'll have to work with vendors and make payments for their services and/or products. They include the Internet service provider as well as your marketing manager and the hardware retailer that supplies you with the equipment are all in that category as vendors. Information that must be completed isn't any different from the information required by customers.

In this book, you'll learn how to create vendors, customers as well as work opportunities in QuickBooks. Additionally, you will be taught how to use the program's vendor, customer and job fields to your company. You'll also learn how to manage jobs, customers and vendor records that you make in QuickBooks.

Create Customers in QuickBooks

Your first job is to convince potential customers to partner with your business. Once you've overcome this issue, you'll be able to move on to create customers in QuickBooks. There are many ways to create a customer account can be found in this:

1. Use QuickBooks Setup. After you've launched the application you will be able to easily access the Setup dialog box to find customer data as well as details of the employee and vendor. It is also possible to get the data via email or just copy and paste it from Excel. If you'd like to add more data into this then return to Setup.

2. One at a time. It is recommended to use"New Customers" if you are looking for customers to be created. However, there are times when you don't have the time to make them individually it is feasible to create them large quantities without having to close the page.

The customers can be added into the system by bulk. It is possible to add or edit Multiple List Entries are useful because they permit you to transfer information from Excel-like programs and transfer data from customers to other. Customer Center Customer Center can be a meeting space for customers and employees alike. It is a place for viewing, creating and alteration of documents, as well as the creation of transactions. Customer Center can be opened in four ways: Customer Center can be opened using four different methods:

1. Pressing CTRL+J even if the application is open

2. Clicking "Customers" on the heading of the Customers tab on the QuickBooks homepage.

3. Start the menu, then press on Customers, and then head through the Customer Center.

4. The icon bar has the "Customers" option. Press the button.

Here's a quick and simple method of creating one customer in QuickBooks:

1. Make use of the toolbar that is included within the Customer Center to create a new customer by completing their job.

2. Within the Customer Name field, enter an identifier or code name that is followed by the naming convention you've picked. The rest of the fields can be ignored as this is the only one that you must complete.

3. To archive the record of the customer and close in the new customer window choose OK. To erase any entries or changes you've made, choose Cancel.

To create an opportunity for a customer shut down the window New Customer, then start the new Job window. It's easier to create all your customers at once and then create jobs for each of them. To assist you in determining what you're looking to complete the Edit and New tabs for customers are divided into sections. Both contact and address information are located in the first section, which is the address information. All fields related to payments are located on the Payment Settings tab. The next tab called Sales Tax Settings can be skipped entirely in the event that your business does not sell tax-exempt items. Next, the Additional

Info tab, which was once a mess of various types of fields, now includes several fields that aren't required such as customers type, sales rep and custom fields that you've designed. The following sections will walk you through each tab, and their respective fields.

Contact Information for entering

If you are planning to invoice your customers, or send them items, or simply check on them, you'll require their address and contact details. This information can be recorded on the new customer's Address information tab. An easy way to fill in this tab:

Company Name Company Name - This is where you enter an option that the application can identify the client, whether it's the name or nickname. Be aware your choice of how to refer to them here will be how they'll appear in invoices, and other documents that you use this application for. When you're finished, QuickBooks will automatically include this name into"Bill To" in the "Bill to" section.

Contact Contact - This is where you input the name of your primary contact, and also the name you would like to address them by to assist in mailing invoices, letters, and other communications between businesses. Note that QuickBooks copies all information you input into the field Invoice/Bill to. It also lets you enter the job's name.

Invoice/Bill to - This is where you'll put the address you want to display in your bills. If you'd like to alter it, you can click the Edit button as well with other options that will allow you to specify your postal code, street as well as street address, among other essential information. Of course, QuickBooks can also copy and paste this information from other sources.

Ship To : If you will not be sending anything to your customer you don't need to fill in this information. However, if you're shipping items, first you'll want to verify whether the billing and shipping address match. If they do it's just a matter of hit Copy and then you're done with it. If they're not it's necessary to enter your shipping information manually.

Payment Information Input

The window for payment settings will show how much you owe, and also how much you'd like to extend your credit of the customer. In these areas, you'll have to enter the customer's details for payment, like:

Account Number. In QuickBooks the account number is completely voluntary. Large accounting software usually assign particular numbers to records of customers that speed the process of finding them. This field acts as an identifier and you must maintain it like the rest of your software for business.

Paying Terms - The part is subject to the conditions you and your client have agreed to adhere to. It's used by the software to define the terms you use to pay your customers, and the terms you've negotiated with your suppliers. This includes the most popular methods that can be helpful in the beginning if you're trying to start your business from the ground but aren't sure about the process. You can also set your own payment terms that will mean you don't have to add the terms each time you use QuickBooks to issue an invoice.

Preferential Delivery Method Choose from mail, e-mail or none to determine a way to deliver information that your client prefers. If you choose E-mail, QuickBooks will automatically activate the checkbox to send emails when you design forms for that particular customer. The Mailing mode shows QuickBooks Billing Solutions which is an additional QuickBooks service that allows you to mail invoices. However, additional charges might be needed. If you would prefer printing the information and send it via the traditional method choose none.

Preferred Payment Method: This permits you to select the preferred method of payment for your client. The drop-down list of options includes but isn't limited to the most popular options, like cash, check or credit card however you are able to add other options should you wish to do so. The method you select will show up instantly when you select the customer for any future endeavors that are useful for clients who return. If a client wishes to pay by an alternative method to the one you've specified choose the desired method from the Receive Payments window.

Information on credit card - In relation to payment with credit cards you are able to provide the relevant details like the name of the card the shipping address and billing code and the date of expiration which could be entered. It is worth bringing to your attention that you can only input only one credit card number per one person.

Credit Limit - Here you are able to define how much credit you'll be willing extend to the customer that you want to extend credit to. If you decide to do this then QuickBooks will alert you whenever an invoice, or order exceeds the credit limit that you set however it won't prevent you from going ahead the purchase, and that is completely your decision. If you aren't planning to follow through without the credit limit It is possible to leave out the values into this field.

Price Level - The majority of companies will have different prices rates for different customers. An excellent example is the fact that not everyone pays the same amount for tickets to the airport. QuickBooks lets you add discount and markups the transactions. You can set up multiple pricing levels and names them in the way you'd like. This allows you to organize your business when it comes to handing markups or discounts. It also makes it simple to use these discounts for all purchase that a particular customer makes.

Include an Online Payment Link on invoices - Invoices with online payment links let customers pay you via Intuit Payment Network. Intuit Payment Network either by paying directly via their banks to yours or using a credit card. (The charges charged for the service differ depending on the method by which users pay). However, the process of setting up this feature takes two steps. The first step is to register for Intuit Payment Network. Intuit Pay Network. If you do not sign up and your customers click on an on-line payment option, they'll be shown an alert that tells them that you've not registered for the service. There's a section in the Payment settings. This is the section you can utilize to tell QuickBooks what payment method to choose for your customer. "Follow Company Default" applies the option you chose in QuickBooks the preferences. Selecting "Always On (bank exclusively)" signifies that the customer is able to pay through the bank account, regardless of the preference of your company. If you select "Always On (bank or credit card)," the customer is able to pay via credit or debit card or through a bank account. "Always Off for this customer" means that QuickBooks does not display the payment option online on invoices for this customer's.

Sales Tax Information Specification

The sales Tax window will show up regardless of whether or not you turned Quickbooks sales Tax on or off it could be quite irritating for certain users. If you don't turn it on, it's practically ineffective. The entire windows will appear by the same grey color, signaling that they're not to be utilized. If you have to pay sales tax, you'll need to select the Tax option under the Tax Code tab and pick the tax rate.

There are many ways to tailor your customer's experience. The following list will demonstrate the fields that you can fill with, and some easy ways they can be utilized:

• Customer type. You can classify customers according to their type. This will make it easier to communicate with customers that are tailored to each type of customer, or determine which ones yield the highest. Once you've created customers with different types, you are able to sort a customer into categories by selecting from the following list. It will show the entries from the customer type list.

* Rep. The addition of a name in this field ties the sales rep to the customer, which could assist in tracking the performance of reps. To ensure that your customers get the best customer service, it's advised to assign a customer service representative to each customer to ensure they are in constant contact with your business regarding the services you offer. When you create the Rep record, you are able to utilize the existing names from your Vendor/Employee or other names list, and, should you prefer to do to do so, create a brand new name for an agent.

* Custom Fields. QuickBooks can provide an unlimited number of custom fields that you can use to input important data that QuickBooks doesn't offer. Because custom fields do not come with a drop-down lists, entries must be completed in a consistent manner.

Additional Contact Information for Customers

While creating the customer's file you'll be able to determine the details about a particular person by using the Address Info tab of the

Create Customer window. You can define the tasks the contacts will are able to perform. In addition, all contacts can be edited and you can remove them whenever you feel best, this is especially helpful in situations where the individuals whom you've saved are either currently in the process of changing jobs change or are already in the process of changing their jobs.

Once you've selected a client You'll be able to view their contact details in addition to having the option of adding additional contacts to their account. This is done by clicking Manage Contacts in the lower right corner and then choosing Add New. Then all you have to do is fill in the information boxes, and any other additional features you want to add. When you're done just click Save and Close , and QuickBooks will quit the application.

Jobs Creation with QuickBooks

If you're in work that is project-based and you know that each job has a beginning and an end point. The same is true for custom-built homes or security systems QuickBooks Job-tracking functions can be utilized to analyse financial performance for each projects.

Let's suppose you wish to know whether you're making cash from the estates in the suburbs or remodeling estates that are low-income as well as the percentages that relate to your rate of success or failure. If you're using QuickBooks for this, it will effortlessly and quickly calculate the financials surrounding it and it's almost similar to having an accountant! Customers and jobs are inseparable from each other within QuickBooks, and it is important to keep an watch on both. Jobs will always remain with the customer. If you attempt to create your job prior to creating an account for a customer, a notification box will pop up telling the user that they must create a basic customer file before you can create the job. Luckily, there are two tabs that can be used for editing and creating customers. both of which contain tabs for information about the customer and job details. In essence, when you create a new customer, you automatically create a job for it, though it is possible to add more jobs later in the event that it's necessary. In the next section, we will guide you through precisely that.

New Job Creation

As was stated earlier that in order to create an employment opportunity, you need to create the customer first. Once you've completed the creation of your customer, follow these easy steps adding a new job the record of a customer:

Then, under the Customer Center's Customers & Jobs tab Click on the right-click icon for the customer whom you want to create a new job, and then choose Add Job from the quick menu. Additionally, you can choose the New Customer and Job tab, then choose New Job. In both instances the new Job window will appear.

* In the box for Job Name in the Job Name box, type in the name of the job. Make sure you choose it carefully and it will be displayed on invoices, or other documents. The maximum length of 41 characters may be entered in this box. The job title must be as brief as well as as detailed as you can both for you and for your customer. In QuickBooks, you can fill out the remainder of the fields for jobs by using the information you provided for the customer to whom the job was made It is only necessary to edit manually the fields in the Payroll settings, Address Information, and Additional

Information. If the address for material for the shipment differs from the address of the customer You will then be asked to fill out the appropriate fields.

* If you want to give additional information regarding the job, click the job Info tab and type in the information in the appropriate fields. If you're adding different types of jobs, it is possible to cross-reference them to other jobs that have similar specific characteristics. It's also not dependent on the type of customer that offered you the job. If you enter information within the section Job Status, it will provide a brief overview of the current events within the Customer Center. If deadlines are an issue for you, then you can calculate the dates of the joband then put them in the appropriate section.

When you're finished with that, press OK. QuickBooks will save the work then close your window.

Vendor Setup

To create an account for a new vendor through the Vendor Center, press CTRL and N simultaneously. You can also make this happen via the menu bar, however, this shortcut simplifies processes. The majority of fields that you'll find are like the customer creation field. This makes the process much easier, as those fields for Customer Name as well as Vendor name function in the exact same manner which makes it more user-friendly. In the same way, QuickBooks advises leaving the Opening Balance field without an entry, and instead , building an entry for the Vendor Balance by inputting invoices and other payments. This could prove very beneficial, particularly when the vendor and the client are the same and are just using different items.

In case you're printing out your bills , as well as all the sheets needed for paying them, then you'll need fill in information about your address and contact details in this field to ensure that QuickBooks will know where to mail the sheets. These fields are very similar to the customer fields. They are also filled in exactly the identical way, so once you've got it down, feel free to move on to payment.

Making Payments

Payments are found in the section on Payment Settings, and while simple to fill out however, are essential and we'll guide you through it, nevertheless.

This Account Number essentially similar to the account number of the customer. In this particular instance, it's reversed. In this case, the vendor gives your business a number rather than vice versa. Once the vendor has given you the number, you only have to input it here. It is essential to keep the number secure and handy. This is due to the fact that there are many blunders that could be committed with it. It also can be used as a proof point when you encounter problems.

Like before you'll select the payment terms that you and the vendor be operating. If you've reached a contract between you and your seller, just enter it in this area, very like the settings for customers.

If you are now unsure as to how your name appears on your cheques, QuickBooks will auto-fill it with the information you have already entered. You can alter it, however, it's generally not recommended.

As with the client side you must input the limit of credit. It is the maximum amount the vendor will provide you with. Simply enter however you want the appropriate amount, and QuickBooks will inform you each when you're trying to go over this limit. This is quite helpful since it allows you to remember your credit limits in your mind.

This level remains exactly the same as the client side , just reversed. If you are in possession of any type of discount that you have with a particular vendor it will be easier to establish it. Instead of sifting through all your data and reducing them by, like, say 10 percent, you could just insert it into QuickBooks and it'll take care of it automatically. This also works for billing employees for their time, so if you charge by seniority, you could have a category for each year that they've worked as well as the amount of increase they've received up to now. This is among the lesser-known abilities of QuickBooks, so it is recommended to utilize it to the maximum extent possible.

Set up of Sales Tax

On the tab for Tax Settings Tab, QuickBooks includes two tax settings. The fields are as follows:

1. Vendor ID. It is only necessary to enter the Social Security number of the vendor or the employer's identification number EIN, short for employer identification, when you are planning to submit 1099 forms for the particular vendor.

2. Vendor suitable for 1099 form. Select this checkbox if plan to make a 1099 to this particular vendor.

When writing a check for future payments or just to verify the changes made to the vendor's credit card, make sure you mark the account on which you wish to make the money. The options for Vendors, such as editing and creation, let QuickBooks to identify which accounts you normally make use of. The most effective way to deal with the issue of accounts for expenses is to allow QuickBooks to read the prior transactions in your financial history. So, whenever you make a record of a payment, a credit card change or a payment for someone else, QuickBooks will generate a new bill based on the entire amount as well as the accounts you chose for the transaction you made.

Additional Information

In the New Vendor windows' tabs The Additional Info tab is a bit spartan and that's probably the reason why it's last in the list. Below are the fields available and the options you have with these fields:

To help you categorize your vendors, QuickBooks has a useful function known as the Vendor Type. It lets you categorize vendors. For instance that you provide every agency you are tax payers in the same tax type, you'll end up more efficient in making your tax filings.

* If you're trying to find various information, you'll need to make use of the custom settingthat lets you set everything by hand. You're able to add seven additional custom fields.

Chapter 2: Sales And Income Selling And Managing

Notifying your clients of the amount that they owe you in addition to deadlines for payment is an essential aspect of accounting. If money isn't coming into your business from outside sources, eventually , you'll shut down your business and end your QuickBooks company's file to the end of time.

Though businesses can use a variety of sales forms to invoice customers invoicing is the most used and, not surprisingly billing customers is commonly known as invoices. The chapter starts by explaining the distinctions between invoices, sales receipts, and statements--each of which are a method to bill customers in QuickBooks, and when they are appropriate for each. Then, you'll be taught how to fill out invoice forms using QuickBooks whether you're invoiced for products, services or both. If you're sending invoices for similar items to a variety of clients (and do not utilize the program's multi-currency option), QuickBooks' batch invoice feature may be helpful. Select the clients then add the items that you'd like to invoice and QuickBooks creates all the invoices on your behalf.

If you manage the billable hours and reimbursements using QuickBooks it is possible to let the program dump these charges into invoices you make.

Then, you'll discover how to handle specific billing issues, such as making invoices for products you offer are backordered. Also, you'll be taught how to make estimates for projects and create invoices when you complete the task. Also, since you may must return funds to clients (like the time they have to return garments made of lime green polyester that suddenly became out of fashion) You'll be taught how to allocate an amount to a customer's account. You can later subtract from an invoice, or refund using checks for refunds or credit to the next invoice from the customer.

The Creation and Sending of Invoices

An invoice is a document that you can use to bill customers for everything, from an app to a loaf bread they purchase from you. If your customers don't pay in full when you offer your product or service or if they make payments in advance, it is important to know how much they owe. Invoices can be used to keep track of the amount your customers are owed by to you (or the accounts payable). Invoices provide all the information regarding the sale, which includes the services you provide or the products you're selling (your products). Invoices also include the quantity and the price or rate for the item. If you require automatic changes to prices (for example, discounts , or markups) invoices will do the job to your advantage.

Based on the version of QuickBooks you are using there are the option of using three different features when making invoices:

* Create Invcices can handle anything that you can put in it, including products, services that are billable, time and even billable expenses. It's included with QuickBooks Pro and higher.

"Create Batch Invoices" allows you select the customers to whom you wish to send the identical invoicing (that that is the exact items and amounts). If you're sending the same invoice to same customers on a regular basis it is possible to create a billing group for these customers. From there on, just select the group. Once you've created the invoice, you are able to send it by email or print to the customers on the list. This feature is included within QuickBooks Pro and higher, provided you don't make use of more than one currency.

* Invoice for Time and expenses, only available on QuickBooks Premier and Enterprise editions it can accomplish everything can the Create Invoices feature is able to accomplish, but it's also an absolute time saver by invoicing for invoiceable expenses and time. It lets you specify a time period and QuickBooks will show you all customers that have invoiced expenses and billable time within the specified time. If you select a client or job, and instruct QuickBooks to generate an invoicefor you, QuickBooks will open an Create Invoices window and fills in the standard fields, and then fills in the invoice table with invoiced time and expenses of the customer. When you're inside the Create Invoices window, you'll be able to add any additional items you'd like to add such as products you've offered discounts on or sold. It also allows you to make batch invoices for costs and time.

Invoices notify your customers about all the details they require to know about the items they bought and the amount they owe. If you have created jobs and customers that have options like tax item, payment terms and sales rep, when you select the customer and job from the"Create Invoices window's Customer job field QuickBooks will fill in the required fields on your behalf.

Receiving Payments

Between performing work or invoicing customers, as well as paying them, you must be aware of who owes you what amount (known by the term Accounts Receivable) and the date when the payment is due. It is possible to add on finance costs to light an ember in your customer's department of accounting, but these charges rarely are enough to compensate for all the effort that you put into collecting late payments. Better are those who make their payments on time and without any reminders, whether mild or other. Because businesses require funds to operate so you'll have to invest the time to keep track of your Accounts Receivable as well as the amount of payments you receive. In this section you'll be taught the basics of keeping track of what customers owe, getting payments directly from them, as well as threatening the customers if they do not pay in time. You'll be able to get started with the Income Tracker an easy dashboard that lets you see estimates you've come up with and the amount customers owe - both due and not paid over the last 30 days. In QuickBooks' collection center, you will identify customers who have overdue or due invoices, collect the necessary information to determine what customers are owed, and make it simple to send reminders. Contrary to invoices sales receipts are the most straightforward and fastest sales forms within QuickBooks. If your customers pay all the way at sale, such as at the retail shop, as an instance, you can create a sales receipt to give the buyer an account of their purchase and the payment. In addition, QuickBooks will send the cash you've earned straight into your account at every bank. (Sales receipts only work when customers make a full payment as that kind of sales receipts can't be used to handle prior customers' balances and payments.) The next chapter will discover how to make sales receipts for a single sales at a time, and also to summarize the day's worth of merchandise.

If you receive cash from a client it is important to record the transaction and declare the invoice paid. When you receive a check the records of accounts receivable are updated and the cash is waiting to be transferred into an account.

1. To be able to receive a payment:

2. Navigate to the menu Customers and click on Receive Payments.

3. In the top section of the form, which includes the name of the client, the amount of payment, mode of payment, as well as the date that the payment was made.

4. Look at the column that is left side of your invoice where you would like to make the money. You may be asked to choose which method to apply the money for any of these scenarios.

5. The excess amount can be an amount that is credited or refunded

6. Underpayments can be left in its current form or erased

7. The customer is left with credit to apply

8. The customer can avail discounts

9. Select the right option and you will be able to see your selections reflected in the totals for selected invoices. If the customer is entitled to credit or discounts available you have the option of deciding which method to apply these credits.

10. Click "Save and Close" or "Save and New" in case you have additional customers' payments to be received.

You can make a choice to ensure that any payments you receive be deposited to the account that you've set up to receive the funds that haven't been transferred at a time, or get automatically calculated and applied when you choose invoices in the list. To create this preference you must go to the edit menu and select Preferences, and then select the tab for Company Preferences in the sales & Customers area

Making Sales Receipts and Sending them

Sales receipts are a form used when you have an offer for which you get paid in full upon completion of sale. Sales receipts may include payment via check, cash, and credit cards.

When your clients are able to pay fully at the time they receive your product or service it is not necessary to record the amount they owe you. But, you may want to keep track of your sale and calculate the tax on sales, or even print receipts of the purchase. In such cases you could create an invoice for sales. Some examples of businesses that utilize sales receipts are cosmetic salons, groomers of pets dry cleaners, as well as restaurants. If you have to keep track of the amount that a customer owes you , or if you did not receive the full amount at the moment of the transaction, do not utilize the sales receipt. Instead, make an invoice as explained earlier in this chapter.

To enter a sales receipt:

1. Navigate to the menu Customers and then click on to enter Sales Receipts.

2. In the top section of this form. It should include Customer's name, Job title Date, Date, as well as the Payment Method.

3. Click on the drop-down for Template and then select the template for sales receipts you'd like to utilize.

4. In the lower part of this form you must enter the purchase details.

5. Save the transaction

You can also make use of the sales receipt to prepare an overview of sales revenue and tax due. You can also summarize the sales for a week or a day in a sales receipt.

Any time, you can access the customer center to view all your customers, as well as those who have balances displayed on the left side of the center. Above the list of customers you can choose to show all customers or customers with balances that are open by choosing from the drop-down boxes under "Customers and jobs." On the bottom part within the Customer Center, you will find a listing of all transactions with your customers. This includes invoices as well as sales receipts, deposits recorded and so on. You can also choose particular types of transactions and certain time periods by with the drop-down boxes that are above the list of transactions which will allow the lists to be updated according to your preferences.

Chapter 3: Bills And Expenses Staffing

While small-scale business owners go through their every day mail in search of envelopes that contain checks, they typically come across more with bills. One issue that frustrates operating a business is that often you have to purchase the products that you offer before you are able to invoice your clients for the items.

If you'd like your accounting records to be correct then you need to tell QuickBooks about the expenses you've made. If you wish your suppliers to remain with you then you must pay them for the bills they've sent. In order to pay for expenses, you can use various forms however QuickBooks can meet the task. This chapter provides options to pay bills (now and later) and provides instructions on how to track invoices and keep track of your payment. If you make a payment immediately then you'll be taught how you can write check checks, utilize credit or debit card or cash in QuickBooks, as well as other alternatives. If you record bills in QuickBooks for later payment and you're learning how you can do about the regular ones and the reimbursable costs and inventory. QuickBooks is here to assist you through each stage of the process: making sure you enter bills that you have received when you'd like to pay them later and setting up bill payment and printing checks that you can send to vendors.

What to do when it comes to managing expenses, you have the option of paying immediately or later. QuickBooks offers features to accommodate both choices. (You can opt to not pay your bills, however QuickBooks cannot assist you with collections agencies or represent your business when it comes to bankruptcy.) Here are the advantages and disadvantages of each method:

Pay them now. If your bills come in every day like meteor showers, make sure you go ahead and pay them each day to ensure you'll be paid on time. In QuickBooks you can pay right away. This involves writing a check recording an account with a debit card or credit card charge and making an on-line payment, or taking money from petty cash, all of which are discussed in the following chapter. If you pay right away it is not necessary to create an invoice in QuickBooks You can just keep track of the expense payment transaction.

• Pay in the future. If your bills come in as regularly like orders from the local coffee shop, you'll likely need to schedule time to pay the bills all at once, so that it doesn't hinder the delivery of services or selling items. Additionally, many businesses don't pay their bills until the day before they're due unless they have a valid reason for it (like the early payment discount). The process of setting up bills from vendors for payment later is known as Accounts Payable, because you can store unpaid charges into an accounts payable account.

In QuickBooks the process of entering bills for later payment offers all the benefits of convenience and effective cash management. It is possible to tell the program when you'd like to pay for bills, such as to avail discounts for early payment or the grace-time period the vendor offers. You can then go about your day without being distracted being aware that QuickBooks will notify you that bills are scheduled to be paid.

Designing and sending Sales Receipts

When you create an entirely new section of QuickBooks it is essential to examine the settings of your company that are related to that particular area. Before entering your Company Settings, you need be sure to understand the different kinds of revenue and sales transactions. Estimates are non-posting transactions which allow you to present your customers with the information you anticipate to be charging them. Consider it an estimate or quote Invoice is the sale transaction you use to let your customer pay by credit card.

An invoice can boost accounts receivable as well as increase income. Payment is the transactions used to obtain the payment due to an invoice. It reduces the balance of accounts receivable and also increases an account with a bank or Undeposited Funds Sales Receipt. The sale is made to receive payments at the time of the sale. It can increase income and boost either a bank account , or the credit of Undeposited Funds Memos which are utilized in situations where a buyer is able to return something or negotiate for a better price.

This results in a credit to the Accounts Receivable account that can be applied to future invoices. Refund receipts can also be used when a client returns something or offers a lower price However, by providing the receipt for a refund you're refunded the payment. Delayed Charges as well as Credits - are offered in Essentials and Plus and are not posting transactions that represent a potential increase in revenue or decrease. They can be utilized on future transactions.

Corporate Settings

Select the Gear icon to open your Company Settings. Four tabs are available on the left-hand side , which allow you to define the settings for how you intend to utilize the company's file. Sales has its own section however, there are additional sales settings in the Advanced Settings.

Customize Sales Forms

The first setting on the Sales tab permits users to personalize your sales form. The modifications are applied to invoices estimates, Sales Receipts, and Estimates. You can choose your style, including uploading your logo.

Go to the Header tab. It allows you to change the titles of your sales form (i.e. you can change an estimate into a quote) Also, determine which fields you would like to be able to view in the Header section , including three fields that you can customize. The Columns tab lets you select the columns you would like to display and arrange them in any order you'd like.

The Footer tab lets you to create a customized message and an additional footer to invoices. The More tab lets you to refine the details. Be sure to check the billable amount of time and expenses when you invoice on the basis of the amount of time or expenses. If the invoice is for time you may include the name of the employee on the form along with groups of activities by time or by type and include the group's subtotaled.

You may also include an accounting summary on the right side of the page. It will show the amount of the balance, the current invoice charges , and the total due. Sales form content lets you set preferences for preferred terms for invoices and delivery methods that can be modified in a sales form. It s setting defaults. It is also possible to include additional line items such as discounts, shipping as well as deposit fields. If you've altered the forms in the past you were able to add three fields to the transaction.

The option to turn this on is in the Sales form's content. The fields can be configured either here or via the page for customization. It is important to note that this is the area where you can indicate whether you would like the fields to be internalor public, or both. Products and Services In this section, you specify whether you wish to show the column for Product/Service or sales forms to ensure that the dropdown menu on your Products and Services List is accessible. In this section, you can switch on the option to track inventory. Inventory is only accessible within QuickBooks Online Plus. Other settings for sales The Messages setting lets you create a the default email content when you email sales forms and also the default message that appears on the form the form itself. Online Delivery settings are related to the way you send your forms to customers and what you would like the customers to view. There are several options for sending in form text in plain text, or making use of Online invoices.

There are a few options to select from when it comes to statements. Advanced settings. Be sure to check the section on Automation in the Advanced settings. Pre-fill forms will ask users if they want QuickBooks to transfer identical information from the previous transaction with that same client. If you enable the option to automatically apply credit, the program will automatically apply any credits that are available to the invoice that follows. Be careful when setting on this (or another automation) preference off.

It could be you're client isn't wish to credit the account on the next invoice instead, they want to apply it to a future invoice. It is possible to set the option to let QuickBooks automatically bill unbilled activities. If you enable this then you will get an email notification on the feed for Activities on the home page. If you wish to charge an estimate from the estimate, it is necessary to switch on the option to copy estimates into invoices. Then, you can choose to only copy accepted estimates, or for pending as well as accepted estimates. It is essential to know the client well and ensure that switching on the Automation settings is appropriate for them. If you notice that your client is experiencing issues with their Accounts Receivable make sure you check these settings.

Find alternative entry points for Entry of Sales Transactions

Customer Center

Customers Center Customer Center, accessed by clicking on Customers in the navigation bar to the left, can be used as a dashboard for creating, editing and review of customers with whom the client of your QuickBooks Online company does business. The list of customers can be exported or printed and can be divided into various categories or filtering. On top of each listing for Customers is a drop-down list where you can create transactions like estimates or invoices or even to send reminders of a due balance or print or mail an invoice. Additionally to batch actions, they can be carried out across the entire list, including printing or sending statements, and sending email directly from QuickBooks Online. Emails can be sent using your preferred online email clients or email programs. Inputting transactions into the Customer Center

Step by Step: Making an Estimate

There are a variety of methods for creating an Estimate using QuickBooks Online. For creating an estimate in the Customer Center Follow these steps:

1. Select Customers on the navigation bar to the left.

2. If required, choose Clear Filter/View All over the Money Bar to produce a complete list of Customers.

3. Choose the drop-down menu on the right column to select the desired customer . Create an estimate.

4. Complete the estimate on screen for the customer you want to work with by entering the desired date, Products and Services of your choice, the quantity of each, the details (override your description, if you wish) and the rate (override your rate, if you wish) from each. and the price of sales tax (check the box to see if tax is applicable on specific items) and choose the sales tax to be applied on the drop-down menu).

5. Complete any other fields you wish to fill in like the Discount or the message to the customer.

6. Choose Save and close, either (by pressing the drop down beside Saving and Close) choose the Save option and then New.

Step by Step: Make an invoice from an estimate

To create an invoice using the Estimate you have just made the simplest method to locate the Estimate is to create it via your Money Bar in the Customer Center.

1. Select Customers on the navigation bar on the left.

2. Select the Estimates rectangle that is located in the upper-left area on the Money Bar. (This results in a list of Estimates that are open.)

3. Locate Cool Cars, for the reason you made that estimate and then click one estimate that is open.

4. In the Transactions listing in the list of transactions, locate the estimate that you'd like to transform into an invoice. Then, choose Start invoice on the far right.

5. Edit the invoice as necessary.

6. Choose Save and close, or (by pressing the drop down adjacent to Close and Save) Close) choose save and new.

A quick reminder Note: If you do not wish to invoice for the entire value of your estimate you can alter the amount as well as the line-items on an invoice. Yet, QuickBooks still considers the estimate as fully paid. There is no invoicing progress for the estimate in QuickBooks Online.

Instructions on how to create an invoice for unbilled activities

You can also easily make invoices for all unbilled activities.

1. Select Customers on the navigation bar to the left.

2. Simply click on the Unbilled Activity rectangle in the left side in the Money Bar. (This allows you to list all unbilled activities.)

3. Take note of the list of unbilled activities and click Start Invoice from here or click here to view any unbilled activities. Select Unbilled Activity for the client whom you would like to see the activity that was not invoiced.

4. Click on Start Invoice.

5. Note: If you are involved in more than one activity listed it is possible to create an invoice that is unique for each one. If you'd like to create a single invoice for all the activities not yet billed you can do this from your Customer Center itself.

6. Include any additional fees such as sales tax, discounts or other charges and save and close.

7. Making transactions available via on the Sales Transactions page (Sales Center)

Step by Step: Make an invoice

1. Select Sales in the Transactions section on the Navigation bar

2. This will open this page. It opens the Sales Transactions or Sales Center. In the Actions column, you will find suggestions for next steps. The Money Bar can be filtered Money Bar here the same as you do use the Customer Center. Additionally, you can add New Transactions at the top right on the page. Click on Invoice

3. Create an invoice with a brand new name for the client you wish to bill. When you type in the

customer's's name QuickBooks displays a drawer on the right that displays the expenses or time that are marked as Billable. It is easy to add them on the bill. The difference between making the invoice here and creating it using the Action column for the person or the an activity is that in this case you are able to choose what you're adding, and the invoice is created using the Action column, it will automatically add the activity that is not billed in the bill.

4. Invoice only for the installation by clicking on Add , and then save & Close.

5. This will bring you back to this Sales Transactions list. Remove the filter so that you can view all transactions. The table below is sorted according to date, however you can sort the table by column headers simply by pressing the heading. If you aren't able to find the columns you want select the Gear icon and select the columns you wish to show.

The Step-by-Step Process: Pay

1. The next step is to get the payment. Let's suppose that your customer paid you a check of

S300. Click Receive Payment under the name of the customer.

2. A list of Outstanding Transactions shows up with the invoice inspected. Deposits can be made into Undeposited Funds as well as directly to an account at a bank. If you're enrolled in QuickBooks Payments, you can use a credit card to make a payment through this site. The details about credit card payments will be covered in the next section of the guide. Choose funds that have not been deposited, in addition to Save as well as Close.

3. On the Sales Transactions page, you can add transactions based upon the current transaction, or make new transactions by using the dropdown to the left of the homepage.

4. Inputing transactions using the Quick Create

5. When you've got the extended view for Quick Create opened, you will see a list of sales-related transactions in the column Customers.

Step by Step Step by Step: Entering Delayed Charge

1. Select Delayed Charge. Delayed charges are non-posting payment and the message you're

sending QuickBooks is that you're required to invoice a client on something specific, however you do not wish to bill for it immediately. For instance, suppose you run a landscaping company and offer gardening services to multiple clients. Each day, you document the when you completed a service on the day, however you only bill once a month. It is possible to record the activity using QuickBooks' Delayed charge and at the end of each month, easily generate an invoice.

2. Enter the name of the customer you want to contact and then in the date field enter W to get to the start in the day. Input the desired service under the product and Services column. Input 4 in the Quantity column and $35 in the column for rate. Save and New

3. Input the name of the client and then in the date field enter K. The plus key. (+). K will bring us to the close of this week, and the + (+) key is advancing the day and brings us to the start of the next week. Input the service performed under the product and service column. Add 3 to the number column and $35 in the column for rate. Click save and Close.

Step-by-Step: How to Create an invoice from Quick Create

1. From Quick Create Select Invoice.

2. Enter the name of the customer. When you type the customer's name If there are not paid (delayed) fees or time that is not billed the drawer will open to the right side so you can quickly add these onto the invoicing.

3. Click on Add All, Save and close.

Step by Step Recurring Transactions

What happens if you've got regular monthly charges that you don't wish to be reminded to enter the charges? Perhaps you'd prefer QuickBooks to create an automatic invoice and then send it out to your clients. Make use of the Recurring transactions feature. The majority of transactions (sales as well as purchases and journal entries) are recurring.

1. From Quick Create, click Invoice.

2. Enter the name of the customer you want to contact and then select the performed service under the heading Product/Service. Set the amount at 1 and the price is $35.00. On the end of the screen, click on Create recurring.

3. The screen will open where you can design an invoice template for recurring use. The template can be named and specify whether you would like to automatically enter it, select to send it automatically or, if you want to schedule it create the schedule. You can save the templates.

4. You can have plenty of freedom when designing templates. Try it out in the template. Be aware that if you've got an already-recorded transaction and wish to set it up as a recurring transaction then open it and select Make Recurring at the lower right of your screen. Keep in mind that most transactions are by recurring.

Step by Step The Recurring Transaction List

1. To look up the list of recurring transactions To view a list of recurring transactions, click the Gear icon and then open Recurring Transactions in the Lists.

2. Here you can make new templates, modify templates already in use, modify or remove.

3. Purchase and Expense Transactions

4. If you are setting up an entirely new section of QuickBooks it is essential to examine the settings of your company that are related to the area. Before you can go into your Company Settings, you need ensure that you are aware of the different kinds of purchase and expense transactions.

5. Bill - a type of transaction you make when you get the bill from a seller but you don't wish to make payment until after. It is included in the Essentials and Plus versions only. expense - a method to record cash, check or credit card transactions.

6. Checks - an option to make transactions less you bank balance. If the transaction is an actual check, you can print checks.

7. Bill Payment - Transaction used to pay the bills that are entered. This feature is included in Essentials and Plus only.

8. Purchase Order - Use the purchase order to notify an agent that you'd like to purchase products or services. It is available through Plus only.

9. Vendor Credit is when you enter an amount of credit from a vendor to account for the

return or refund from an individual vendor. It is only available only in Essentials and Plus.

10. 10. Credit Card Credit - this transaction shows a credit card reimbursement from a seller

11. Each of these transactions is related to the transfer of money. Certain of these transactions may be initiated from multiple access point, while others can be launched from only one.

12. Find the appropriate settings for expenses.

13. Corporate Settings

14. Hit the Gear icon to open your Company Settings. You will find four options on the left-hand side , which allows you to define the settings for what you intend to do with the company's file. There is a separate category for expenses and there are expenses settings in the Advanced Settings. These preferences let you to utilize products, track purchases made by the client and make them to be billable. Be aware that whether you are able to make use of these features depends on the level of your subscription. This is also the place to enable Purchase Orders. In the Advanced tab, you'll find the same automation options that we have

seen when dealing with customers. Do you wish that QBs automatically make payments to bill payers? Take a moment to think about this before you switch it on. Under the Miscellaneous section it's recommended to switch on double check as well as the bill warnings.

15. Find alternative entry points to entering transactions for purchasing

Vendor Center

Vendor Center: The Vendor Center, accessed by clicking on Vendors in the navigation bar to the left It is a dashboard that allows adding or editing vendors and for reviewing them that clients of the QuickBooks Online company does business. This List of Vendors can be exported or printed and can be divided into various categories or filtering. On top of each Vendor listing is an Action column, which includes an option drop-down menu from which to generate transactions such as cheques or bills, or remove a vendor from active. Additionally, you can send emails to vendors in bulk through this Batch Actions drop-down menu. The emails will be sent using the web-based email or email clients.

Step by Step: Making an Act

1. Within the Action list, select Create a bill for the selected customer. Note: Due to the settings for the company you can choose to direct transfer money to an account in the account chart, or select an item from the Products and Services List or combination.

2. In the Account information, enter Advertising for $2,500, payable to the customer for which you carried out the said advertisement.

3. Utilize this keyboard shortcut, Ctrl + Alt + S.

4. Create a second bill for a different customer that you would like to pay for the example of Meals and Entertainment, $250.00 and then save and Close.

5. Note that when you type the keyboard shortcut QuickBooks keeps the transactions in its database and presumes you'd like to make an additional entry that is the same kind. However, QuickBooks does not presume that you want to work with the same vendor. So in this particular instance you must enter another customer in the Vendor Center as the vendor. In the Vendor Center now shows two open bills for the customer.

Step-by-Step Paying bills

1. In the column called Action Click on the Make Payment button next to the name of the client. QuickBooks will open to the Bill Payment screen with the outstanding bills and a checks marked to pay. On near the bottom of the page, you have the option to select to pay with a the bank account or credit card.

2. Then at the bottom of the screen , click on Save and then close.

3. Like the Customer Center where you can click on the name of the vendor and obtain the list of transactions you can take action on or make new transactions by selecting the drop-down list to the right.

4. Entry of Transactions -> Costs

5. As you've learned that if you click the tab Expenses, under Transactions on the navigation bar QuickBooks displays a list of the last 365 days ' worth of transactions. The screen can be filterable to change the look of the screen. It is possible to drill down on any transaction. You can also make an entirely new transaction and print your checks.

The Step-by-Step Guide to Entering the Expense Type of the Transaction

1. In the new Transaction drop-down menu, choose the category of expense. To summarize what was mentioned earlier, an Expense kind of transaction permits you to either decrease your bank account , or increase the amount of credit card you can charge to make a purchase for the business. This is a great option to serve your "shoebox" customers. They bring in a bag of receipts from expenses that have been marked with whether they made use of the check, credit card or cash. Instead of having to sort through them, and then put them in piles according to the payment method, you could simply input the information on the screen for expenses.

2. Enter an amount for the vendor you want to use. The transaction was processed using the help of a Mastercard and was for Dues and Subscriptions of $10.

3. To the right of the screen, select Save as well as New.

4. Input a transaction for one vendor. It was paid through checking using manual check

number 32. This was to pay Commissions and Fees for $100. Save and close.

5. In the Expense Transactions page, both expenses are shown, but one of them affected the bank account while the other one a credit card. If you're making all checks, you should use the Check feature instead of the expenses transaction.

Step-by-Step Paying Multiple Charges

1. In the past, you have learned to pay for one bill at one time. The bill was paid through your Vendor Center and it also can be paid through your Expense Transactions section. If you wish to pay multiple bills to multiple vendors at once You must access Pay Bills using Quick Create.

2. Click to Quick Create and select Pay Bills.

3. Choose Checking as the payment Account.

4. Select the bills to pay, and then enter the date for payment, and select the payment method printed Check.

5. Notice that in the upper right hand corner you can sort the list according to how you would like to view the bill list. Click Pay Bills.

6. If you choose"Pay and Print," QuickBooks provides you with the list of all bills that have been paid and print the checks. If you've chosen to pay using Printed Check however, you didn't print them yet and they're batch printed, something will be explained in the coming days.

The Step-by-Step Guide: Make an Check (write the check to pay for a bill)

1. Click for Quick Create and then select the option to Check.

2. Enter the name of the vendor. For example Diego's Road Warrior Bodyshop. If you type in a vendor's name, and there's an outstanding charge for the company, then a drawer will pop onto the right-hand portion of your page. This lets you include the invoice in the form of a check. The effect of accounting is to lower the bank accounts as well as reduce the Accounts payable. This feature can to prevent customers from making the error that they write a cheque against an invoice already paid and then posting it into expenses accounts.

3. To add the invoice to the Check, click Add. This change the transaction type from Bill Payment to Check. Close and Save.

4. If this check wasn't meant to cover an outstanding debt Enter the account number or the item's details.

Step-by-Step Printing Checks in batches

1. Click the Quick Create and then Print Checks.

2. You'll need to make sure that your cheques are aligned. If they're lined up vulnerable to marking them to print.

3. Choose which prints you want to print, then preview and print. Before you print you'll have to verify that the start number of the check is correct.

4. Transactions = Banking

5. The Banking Center allows you to connect your bank and credit cards to QuickBooks. Once you have done that, QuickBooks will download transactions automatically every night but you can also manually download them by clicking Update in the upper right-hand corner.

Step-by-Step: How to Use the Center for Banking Center

1. On the left side of Transactions on the Navigation bar Select Banking.

2. On on the right side of your screen linked accounts for credit and bank accounts are shown in addition to the amount of transactions downloaded and must be filled in or match. Even though QuickBooks downloads transactions on a regular basis You can select Update to import the most recent transactions.

3. If your bank account can do not have a connection to QuickBooks the dropdown of the Update icon lets you import CSV or QFX, QBO, and OFX formatsted documents. You can connect accounts by clicking the icon beside an Update symbol. Another option in the Update drop-down menu is to set up and manage rules. It's possible to do this after you've learned the various components within the Banking Center. In the middle is a tab to display New Transactions, In QuickBooks and Excluded.

4. Recent transactions: These are new downloaded transactions. These are the ones should be taken action on.

5. In QuickBooks the QuickBooks database, there are transactions that were added or matched to within the New Transactions tab. While there isn't any within the file sample, when you have started making use of Banking

Center Banking Center in a live file, you will find several transactions listed in there.

6. Not Included: These are transactions you've decided not to add to QuickBooks. Most often, this is since they've already reconciled and entered. Consolidated transactions already entered won't be displayed as an actual match. This usually happens when you first use Banking Center. Banking Center.

7. A list of downloaded transactions appears in the next section on the screen. The default setting is to display all downloaded transactions, however there is the tab Recognized transactions. They are those that either matched or QuickBooks has predicted the type of transaction you'd like to input the information using previous transactions and the rules. It is possible to address the first ones to tidy up your list. Look to the left there's the Printer icon as well as an icon for Gear. Print the list of transactions.

8. Select the Gear icon. You can choose preferences regarding the columns you wish to see as well as the number of rows you would like to see on the Banking Center.

9. Click Copy Description. This function instructs QuickBooks to copy the description of the transaction from the bank into in the Memo field. The Memo field will show in reports. It's also helpful in helping to troubleshoot entries. It is possible to edit the memo prior to adding it to QuickBooks. Transactions can be classified using any column. When as you move down you will notice that within the match list you can see that QuickBooks has already identified numerous transactions.

10. Simply click on the header of the column. category or Find a match.

11. QuickBooks will automatically search for matches. The match could be made against an invoice, check or deposit, or a check received by the customer, and so on. After a quick examination, you're in agreement that they match, you can do so each transaction in turn by clicking on match within the action list. Alternately, if you wish to enter multiple transactions simultaneously, choose the first transaction you'd like for entry, keep the shift key down, and then select the final transaction you wish to enter. To do this, click the down arrow for Batch actions, and then accept the

selected. This matches the downloaded transaction to a transaction already recorded in QuickBooks.

12. Click on the selection box to select Hicks Hardware. Press the shift key and then click on the box to select Hall Properties. When you press your shift button, QuickBooks selects all the transactions between Hicks Hardware and Hall Properties.

13. Choose the batch Actions drop-down menu, and then select Accept Selected. These transactions will be moved away from in the New Transactions tab and onto the QuickBooks tab.

14. Return to your New Transactions tab and click on the column header to display Description. The expense report contains two transaction for A Rental. QuickBooks cannot determine the name of the vendor nor the account that it should use.

15. Input A Rental in The Payee field. There is no entry within QuickBooks of A rental. You can add it as vendor.

16. Choose Equipment Rental as the account to post the transaction. Once you have done this,

QuickBooks assumes you want the second transaction to A Rental to use the A Rental vendor and post to Equipment Rental. You can create each transaction separately or simply click on the selection boxes, and then under the section called Batch Actions Select Accept Selected like you did previously in this exercise. If you're looking to spl t the transaction , you can do it easily by clickir g Split.

17. Find the vendor at the top on the screen. QuickBooks doesn't know the location to place this transaction.

18. Select the update dropdown and then select Manage Rules

19. Click on the New rule.

20. Input the vendor's name as the rule name within the description field.

21. Choose the vendor you want to use as the Payee and the Supplies as the category.

22. Click Save.

23. Select Bank and Credit Cards.

The vendor is now showing Supplies as the account used to post and indicates that the account was created according to a set of rules. This rule was simple. You can make some complicated rules. For instance, if a vendor's value is less than $500, then post it to Supplies. Create a second rule that says in the event that the vendor's value is more than $500, then post to Equipment. It is also possible to make rules for splits. For example, a company's transactions must be split 40 percent Internet and 60 percent to Telephone. If you click on a transaction from the Banking Center there are three radio buttons.

You've been working using Add. If you believe there could be a match, switch the button radio option to find match, and QBs will attempt to find matches between the transactions. If it's impossible to find it like we mentioned earlier it could be due to the fact that the transaction was already reconciled within QBs. If that's the case and you're not able to add the transaction since it's already in QBs, click the box, and then under Batch Actions section, choose Exclude selected. The Transfer button will declare that the transaction is an exchange between two accounts of a company.

Find Additional Transactions that were initiated using the Quick Create Menu

There are various other types of transactions that are accessable via using the Quick Create function. One instance where transactions can only be accessable via Quick Create function is time tracking. The ability to track time can be achieved through time tracking using the Single Time Activity or the Weekly Timesheet function. This feature is available even if you're not enrolled in QuickBooks Online Payroll.

Step-by-Step to fill out a single Time Activity

1. Choose the Quick Create (+) at the top of the QuickBooks Online window.

2. If needed, choose Show More.

3. Under Employees, select single time activity.

4. Name the employee or Vendor whose hours are being recorded.

5. Input the date for the day that time is being recorded. 6. Enter the customer who is the one whose time is being tracked.

6. Enter the Service that will be rendered at this point.

7. If the Billable preference is switched on, make sure you can bill for the period as well as the cost of billing.

8. Input the time you are tracking such as 3.5 hours in either HH:MM format (3:30) or decimal format (3.5). Check that box beside Enter Start & End Times and complete the fields to indicate Time of Start Time as well as End Time.

9. Give a an explanation of the task you've completed.

10. Choose Save and close, or (by pressing the drop down adjacent to Close and Save) Close) choose save and new.

The Step-by-Step Guide: Complete an Weekly Timesheet

1. Choose the Quick Create (+) at the top of the QuickBooks Online window.

2. If needed, choose Show More.

3. Under Employees, choose Weekly Timesheet.

4. Input the full name and address of the employee or Vendor whose time is recorded.

5. Input the week of work that the time is being recorded (the preferred day for the first day of

the work week for this business is set in the company settings for Time Tracking).

6. In every row of the weekly Timesheet grid, you must enter the name of the individual whose time being tracked as well as the Service that is being provided at this time and the amount of time that was recorded day-to-day during the week in either the format of HH:MM (e.g. 3:00) as well as in decimal format (e.g., 3.5). If you are required to enter it for billing purposes, you must enter in the Bill @ rate, and the tax-paying status.

7. Choose Save and close, or (by selecting the dropdown menu adjacent to Close and Save) Close) choose save and new.

Step by Step How to Make a Bank Transfer

1. Choose the Quick Create (+) at the top of the QuickBooks Online window.

2. If you are required, click Show More.

3. Under Other, select Bank Deposit.

4. Choose which account at the bank you will use for the deposit.

5. Input the date.

6. If there are funds in Undeposited Funds the funds will be displayed at the top of the display.

7. Choose the existing payments if they're part of your deposit.

8. The Add New Deposits section, include any other transactions you have received in the Add New Deposits area, usually not related to sales transactions.

9. If you're taking cash back from your deposit, you need to click on the account that you posted to, (i.e., Petty Cash or Owner's Draw) and select the amount of cash to be taken.

10. Click Save and close or Save and Close. Then click New.

11. You could also print a Deposit Summary and Slip using Deposit slips that are preprinted or a Summary Only that you could make on plain white paper.

12. You can make a check for any expense you can track using QuickBooks expense accounts, and also for any non-inventory item service, or other charges. If you're making use of purchase orders or inventory and purchase orders, you

can also write checks for inventory items as well.

13. To write a check:

14. Click on the Banking menu and select Write Checks.

15. Click on the Bank Account drop-down menu and select the account that you wish to issue the check. If the bank hasn't yet been established in QuickBooks and QuickBooks will request for you to create to the list of new vendors. If the vendor has been added to the list of vendors and the address was given, QuickBooks will automatically fill in the address for the vendor on the check.

16. Complete the check on screen the same way as you would with fill in a paper check.

17. List your expenses (shipping costs, taxes or any other costs not connected with one particular item) in your Expenses tab.

18. If you're purchasing items to stock your inventory, you can enter the items into the Items tab.

19. Once you've entered the necessary details, click "Save and Close" or "Save and New" in

case you have additional check to make. You can also make use of your "Previous" as well as the "Next" menu buttons at the upper left corner to look at checks that you have written

20. To print and find one check:

21. The blank check form should be loaded onto the printer.

22. Navigate to the Banking menu, and then click Write Checks.

23. Click Find and type in the name of the check you wish to print.

24. Double-click to open the check you'd like to print.

25. Click Print.

26. The Checks window, click Print. Checks window, select the options you prefer and then click Print.

Entering Bills

At first , the process of entering bills into QuickBooks and paying them later could appear like more work than simply making checks. But , as you'll see in this chapter, there are many advantages to entering bills into QuickBooks.

Additionally, the program makes it very simple to pay them.

You should pay bills as soon as you receive the bills and then pay them later. Utilize to use the Enter Bills window for entering of bills at receipt. After that, make use of your Pay Bills window for payment of the bills. It is possible to set up QuickBooks for you to notify you of the payment your bills as they must be paid. This way it allows you to keep your cash in your company to the maximum extent you can. You may still need to make use of a check to pay the invoice, but this method lets you track the amount of money owed. In addition you are able to examine reports that analyze the unpaid bills to find out information the names of vendors to whom are owed money. Don't just create a check through the Write Checks window to pay for bills you have entered into the register for accounts payable or in the Enter Bills window. Make use of your Pay Bills window to pay the bills.

"Click on" the "Enter Bills" icon on your homepage. Once you click, the "Enter Bills" window will appear to enter your bill.

Note: Enter the necessary details about the vendor dates, due date and bill due date, into the Bill template. (If the vendor isn't already setup in QuickBooks and you are required to setup it here).

Similar to writing checks The two tabs beneath the Bill template let you connect the bill to specific expense accounts or particular items. You can choose either the item or account selecting the drop-down menu that appears or simply type into the expense account or item, and then enter the information exactly the same way as you would when writing checks.

* If the bill is linked with an account or item that have not yet been created in QuickBooks You can make them by choosing "Add New" and adding the account or item.

After you have finished entering all of the necessary information, you can click "Save and End" or "Save and New" in case you have additional bills to add.

Make sure that it is set up to notify you of your due bills if you want to be regularly reminded. Select Edit - Preferences in the toolbar. Select "Reminders" in the lower left preference list and then click"Company Preferences" from the drop-down menu "Company preferences" tab. You can alter the settings of reminders, such as the timeframe for reminders.

Paying bills

Inputting bills into QuickBooks isn't the same thing as paying bills. The invoices you record in your company's file will record the amount of money you owe as well as when however they don't do anything to pay your suppliers. Pay bills will be your QuickBooks feature that lets you send your money to the banks. You can choose the bills you wish to pay, the amount you'll have to pay on each along with the payment method, the account, and the date. If you have credit or early payment discount, you can add them, as well.

You can click"Pay Bills "Pay bills" symbol on your home page. When you click on the icon, the "Pay Bills" window will be displayed, giving you the list of all the bills you have entered.

* Choose the bill or bills that you would like to pay, as well as the date of payment and payment method and the account you use in

order to settle your bill(s). If you are paying by check, you may choose to print checks with QuickBooks, or specify the number of the check on the check you wrote. QuickBooks will reduce the balance on your account for checking by 17 percent of the amount of the bill that was paid. If you made a payment using credit or debit card QuickBooks increases the balance that you owe to your credit card in line with the payment bills.

* Click "Pay selected bills" then QuickBooks will create an electronic check (if you chose to use a checks as the method of payment) and update the accounts associated with it to reflect the payment.

* You don't have to open the Pay Bills window in order make payments. You can make checks or credit card transactions and cash expenses directly into an appropriate account. If you do enter bills using the Enter Bills window or through the accounts payable register then you must make use of Pay bills to make the payment of your bill. You should not make use of to use the Write Checks option to settle a bill you entered using either or both of the methods.

Any time you are able to access the vendor center to view the entire list of vendors and the ones with which you have balances on the left-hand corner of the center. Below the list of vendors you can opt to see all vendors, or only those with whom there are balances open using the drop-down menu beneath "Vendors." The lower section within the Vendor Center you will find a list of all transactions made with vendors, including invoices or bill payment, checks as well as other transactions. You can also choose certain types of transactions as well as particular time frames through the drop-down menus above the list of transactions.

Chapter 4: What's Quickbooks And How Can Businesses Make Use Of It?

QuickBooks is a small-business accounting software that businesses utilize to manage costs and deals and keep track of exchanges that occur daily. It can be used to receive clients, pay bills, create reports for organizing, cost recording and that's only the beginning. The QuickBooks product line includes several arrangements that work great for anyone whether a solopreneur or an enterprise of a reasonable size.

There are several QuickBooks options, it's crucial to choose the best one. Prior to submitting, you can take QuickBooks to test it by using a free 30 day trial. The trial is an experimental version of QuickBooks which lets you explore all of the bells and bells. The most appealing aspect is that there is no need for a credit card.

What are the smallest businesses that use Quickbooks for?

Small businesses usually utilize QuickBooks to manage their invoices, pay costs, and keep track of their earnings. It is also used to prepare budgetary month- and year-end reports, just like they prepare for annual or quarterly costs for their business. It is common for business owners to run QuickBooks by themselves or use an outsourced or in-house bookkeeper.

The top eight QuickBooks small-scale businesses use are:

1. Control Income and Sales

You can control your salary and deals through QuickBooks, by creating invoices that follow deals made with the client. You can determine if customers have to pay you (also known as the balance of your receivables in your records) by reviewing the Accounts Receivable Aging Report that contains the details of both the current as well as past due bills. This is an example of the Aging Report that comes from QuickBooks.

Large companies will want to examine QuickBooks Premier or QuickBooks Enterprise depending on the amount of clients they require.

How Many Users Do You Really Need?

The amount of clients you require will aid in determining the right software for your company. Examine this graph to determine which software is best suited to your business size.

Note: This diagram illustrates the largest number of QuickBooks clients compatible with every QuickBooks version and may require additional fees.

What Accounting Experience Do You Have?

If you don't know about accounting, you'll have to stay clear of QuickBooks Pro, Premier, or Enterprise unless you're willing to accept the effort to learn.

QuickBooks Online or QuickBooks Self-Employed are two of the simplest alternatives to learn about when you don't have a lot of knowledge or aren't able to keep changing the book.

In the event that you're an accountant, or someone who has extensive accounting expertise You might like the challenge of QuickBooks work areas as they adhere to increasingly conventional accounting procedures.

2. Monitor the status of bills and expenses

QuickBooks automatically monitors your expenses and costs , as it associates with your banking and Visa information with QuickBooks and the majority of your expenses are recorded and categorised. If you need to track an order for a money exchange or check and you want to record it in QuickBooks within a matter of seconds.

QuickBooks can also assist you pay your expenses when they are due. For example, you can ensure that you are able to pay your bills in time through the use of an account

Accounts Payable Report is under two minutes. This report will reveal the information on your current and past due invoices so you are able to resolve any issues swiftly. Here is an example of the A/P Aging Report that comes from QuickBooks.

Sample Aging Summary Summary Report for A/P created by QuickBooks

3. Improve Key Reporting Information for your business

If you handle the entire flow of money and outflow activities within QuickBooks and QuickBooks, you will be able to get access to some reports that offer significant bits of insight into your company. The majority of reports are created in QuickBooks and are able to be executed in just two clicks. reports are refreshed as you input and save transactions.

This could be helpful in the event that you need to present the financials to an investor or to your bank in exchange for an independent venture loan or credit extension. Additionally, with you can use the Accounts Receivable Report as well as Accounts Payable Report are both useful. Acccunts Payable Report which we have discussed previously are the most important three reports will help you assess the general health of your business:

• Profit and Loss Statement

*Balance Sheet Report

• statement of cash flows

Below, you'll find an in-depth description of each report along with an example of what it will look like in QuickBooks.

The Profit and Loss report

The report on profit and loss can be completed in some minutes. It will show you the amount of profit you earn by analyzing your earnings in terms of the expenses. It provides you with your principal goal of in total earnings (loss) in a certain period of time, such as one month, seven days or the quarter. This is an income and loss Report from January 1 through September 29, 2016 for a fictional business, Paul's Plumbing:

Example Profit and Loss Statement created by QuickBooks

Balance Sheet Report

A balance sheet reveals the assets, liabilities and Equity for an organization at a particular moment in time. In just a couple of snapshots, you can produce the balance sheet report using QuickBooks. Here is a screenshot of the Balance Sheet report on September 29, 2016 for an ingenuous organizationcalled Paul's Plumbing:

A sample Balance Sheet Report of the Balance Sheet from QuickBooks

The Statement of Cash Flows

It is easy to create an income statement using QuickBooks. This report will inform each of the procedures that affect working financial, contributing and cash flow and money outflows for your business. This is a sneak preview of the income statement for the months of January through September 2016 for an invent company, Paul's Plumbing:

Example statement of cash flow taken from QuickBooks

4. Run Payroll

Payroll is an area that you'd prefer not to delay in trying to manually calculate it. Making mistakes when calculating the checks could lead to severe penalties and make you unsatisfied. To assist, QuickBooks has its very own payroll system which can calculate and manage payroll as often as you'd like.

The greatest benefit of using QuickBooks payroll is that it's integrated with QuickBooks which means that your budget reports will be up-to-date with the most current payroll run. The purchase of the QuickBooks Payroll membership necessary in order to use the most current charges for payroll to determine the business and representative payroll costs.

Some of the advantages of running your payroll using QuickBooks include:

* Pay representatives using a check or by directing the to the store

* State and federal pay rates are determined by nature.

* QuickBooks will fill in your payroll tax forms for you

* You can pay by e-check directly via QuickBooks

5. Track Inventory

If you must keep track of the inventory that you sell, like close by sums, close by sums, and costs per unit, QuickBooks will naturally track and refresh the information in exchanges. In QuickBooks you will find several reports available to help you manage your the inventory.

While it is possible to track inventory with the Excel spreadsheet, this can turn out to take a ot of time. This is an example of Inventory Valuation Summary Report that comes from

QuickBooks. This report lists a listing of your inventory items and the quantity available, the normal cost, and tne total value.

6. Make Taxes Mcre Effective

If you're still not convinced that QuickBooks can reduce your expenses using QuickBooks, think about the amount you're worried about during cost season to be. No matter if you want to connect a couple of Excel spreadsheets or put together the receipts in a shoebox and tax forms, it could take longer to provide your tax accountant the information they require than it will take to create your own government tax form!

At Fit Small Business, we employ QuickBooks Online to deal with the entire company's accounting and tax needs. We've created a tax expert with a customer ID and secret key for access to our QuickBooks information . They can then access the data needed to create our assessment forms. Since everything is tracked in QuickBooks, we do not have to have to spend a lot of time separating the bank statements and receipts. This does not only guarantee that we've recorded all costs and salaries and expenses, but it also increases accuracy.

7. Accept Online Payments

One of the best ways to increase your revenue is to give customers the option of paying their invoices via the internet. With QuickBooks you can incorporate Intuit Payments. Intuit Payments feature with a just a click.

If activated, all of your client invoices you send out through email will contain the "Pay Today" button. The recipient can click the catch to pay the invoice using any major charge card , or by entering the bank account details to authorize an ACH payment straight from the ledger.

There is no month-to- cost to use Intuit Payments. You pay per exchange in the following manner:

*Bank Transfers (ACH) - - Free

* Card Scrubbed * Card Swiped 2.4 percent, plus 25 pennies

* Card Invoiced * Card Invoiced 2.9 percent in addition to 25 pennies

* Card Keyed in - 3.4 percent in addition to 25 pennies

3. Scan Receipts

Another crucial aspect that makes charging time easy is the ability to organize your receipts within QuickBooks. All QBO customers have the option of downloading QuickBooks on their cell phones. They can download the QuickBooks App to their cell phone for free, take an image of a receipt and then transfer it to QBO within a couple of minutes.

No more lost receipts, or having to physically link your receipts with downloaded bank exchanges. QuickBooks lets you add an invoice to the bank exchange you are comparing! You can save an unlimited amount of receipts into QBO to be stored in the cloud, along with the information you have. This is extremely helpful for companies that have to track a lot of expenses, such as law firms and lawyers.

Why choose QuickBooks?

QuickBooks isn't without competition:

* Xero

* FreshBooks

* Sage 50 (Previously called Peachtree)

* Account Edge

* Wave

* Others...

In addition, people frequently have me answer the question: "Why QuickBooks and not an alternative program?" Or "Other than QuickBooks which are my options to use an accounting software?"

Since I'm not a customer of any other program which isn't QuickBooks I am unable to make an analysis of features by features However, I will make reference to the bullet points that explain the reasons I suggest QuickBooks without hesitation to my clients, instead of looking into an alternative arrangement:

* QuickBooks is available in a variety of "flavors": QuickBooks Online Simple Start, QuickBooks Online Essentials, QuickBooks Online Plus, QuickBooks Mac, QuickBooks Pro, QuickBooks Premier, and QuickBooks Enterprise. This means that we have plenty of flexibility when the evaluation, inclusions the

preferred method of working. With both a CLOUD as well as an DESKTOP arrangement.

• Mobile and iPad likeness The two versions Online as well as Windows versions provide alternatives to mobile and tablet interfaces (restricted obviously) to make certain exchanges when in and around.

• Online banking (Bank Fees) The majority of banks in the US offers an QuickBooks trade option, which accelerates data section as well as bank compromise exponentially , compared to the 100% manually-constructed Information section frameworks. Some accounting programs do not offer these options.

Accounting Support The majority of CPA's and Tax preparers in the open practice have support for QuickBooks, and can request an QB file to carry out their tasks. Other accounting frameworks might not be compatible with smaller or less specific CPA companies. In addition, accountants receive specific tools in Accountant's version of QuickBooks which can speed up the accounting process.

* Many QuickBooks Consultants: There are 60k plus people who are part of in the Intuit

ProAdvisor Network, and it's easy to locate nearby experts throughout the US to allow customers to organize/arrange or back QuickBooks.

* Community Support If you search "QuickBooks training practice" on YouTube You will find numerous videos that will help you learn QuickBooks on your own. The Intuit Support site: http://support.quickbooks.intuit.com/has huge amounts of technical information. The people group Support site: https://community.intuit.com/has additionally huge amounts of Q&As commonly asked and replied by clients.

"Local Training: just like the rest of us, you can find a lot of advisors in the area as well as Community Colleges educating QuickBooks courses in addition to there is no accounting software like QuickBooks.

* Third Party Applications: QuickBooks hosts the biggest database of good third-party applications that can import and share information between QuickBooks and other accounting frameworks such as CRM, Workflow

Management, Shopping Carts, Inventory, and other such applications.

* Payroll Support: There are a lot of accounting software which don't support Payroll or it's manual procedure. QuickBooks comes with EFTPS installment computerization, as well as IRS structure filling in.

We hate receiving the phone call that the customer's Pro or Premier record has been omitted from their organizational document. We must have the record corrected by Intuit. And they must upgrade into QuickBooks Enterprise at any rate! Review the size of your file by pressing ctrl +. If you're moving towards 100,000 - 80,000KB, it is time to look at Premier Pro. From 100,000KB to 120,000KB, it's an ideal time to move up to Enterprise.

Help when You Need It's a unique deal with a one-year subscription, ES gives the ability to connect with U.S. - based item experts, unlimited expert assistance upgrade, as well as online backup.

* Employee Organizer: Use the implicit HR tool to track date of the contract, dates for firing and raises, the expected set of responsibilities

as well as notes with the date stamp and period to keep track of the most representative aspects.

Pricing/Value: do not know the pricing concept for the exact evaluation of all accounting programs available, but I do know the amount of features offered in comparison to the value connection. You can buy QuickBooks Pro for around $180 at Amazon or QuickBooksPrice.com It typically lasts for three years with no the need for an upgrade.

* QuickBooks is extremely adaptable and allows each business's needs to modify it to meet the specific needs of. From tracking inventory levels to preparing unique invoices and measures, QuickBooks adjusts to your particular needs.

Simple accounting duties can be easily saved in the software that saves you valuable energy and time. For instance, many banks and Visas can join QuickBooks to download exchange data without manual input and blunders.

The installed customer base for QuickBooks is so extensive it has been extensively tested and is completely stable and stable. If you consider all the features and functions of the product with regard to the cost there is virtually no comparable product available at this point that provides a better incentive to private businesses.

* QuickBooks is perfect for a variety of vertical market apps that allow programs for the industry afterward to import directly into QuickBooks and a larger number of these programs are added regularly. Examples include: Point of Sale, Construction, and Medical and more. In addition QuickBooks Premier Edition has been expanded to include Construction, Point of Sale and Medical. QuickBooks Premier Edition has been made explicit to be used in industry models.

In the wake of realizing that many private firms have or in the near future they will be able to exceed the capabilities that are available in QuickBooks, Intuit released its innovative software called QuickBooks Enterprise Solutions, which lets larger businesses to make use of QuickBooks Enterprise Solutions. For example, QuickBooks Enterprise Solutions is an ideal fit for companies with 100-200 representatives and $10 million in transactions that allow access to as many as 20 concurrent clients.

* QuickBooks offers a range of unique reports that are able to be produced at any point that you're trying to determine the way your business is moving ahead. All of your data is gathered together to provide an overall view of your company's health.

• Save money by using QuickBooks. You're choosing a low-cost program that allows you to work with every aspect that make up your company in a sound manner.

The customer base of QuickBooks indicates that it's an efficient, reliable accounting software. Numerous companies from all over the world have opted for QuickBooks and the number of customers continues to grow.

* QuickBooks allows data that is imported into a variety of famous applications, such as for instance the Microsoft Office Suite. Other independent applications for companies and other products have been developed to integrate data in a consistent manner into your QuickBooks program.

QuickBooks can assist in the development of your business through the creation of an action plan to ensure you are on the right course and achieve your goals. This strategy can be utilized to get small business credit or to sort out assets for extensions in the future.

QuickBooks as with all accounting program, is an instrument. In the same way, purchasing tools for carpentry will not transform someone who is just beginning to learn into an expert, neither will one of the accounting programs is independent of others to effectively handle your company. In this way similar way, as with the majority of abilities, there's no substitute for knowledge and knowledge and. My QuickBooks programming knowledge is backed through my long-standing involvement in bookkeeping, financial detail, tax assessment along with business consulting services for many different projects. This is a huge chance to help you , the business owner, implement a productive QuickBooks setup for your business.

Some of the ways I can help you with QuickBooks is:

Implementing programming, arrangement and a plan for a suitable bookkeeping for your business.

The issues that arise when the introduction and operation of QuickBooks using multi-client modes on the system.

You are constructing or altering an existing diagram of documents that is suitable for your particular business.

Deciding to open adjusts is not always a straightforward process especially when you are moving to a manually-managed bookkeeping system.

I am reconciling a line of interest receivable or payable, stock, and finance registers with an overall record.

I have laid out an organized process to move in your current structure to QuickBooks.

I am establishing client stock, seller, costing of employment, and finance documentation and design documents.

I am customizing the structure and reports.

Fixed resource valuable detailing.

I am integrating vertical-market applications into QuickBooks.

Examining the present QuickBooks arrangement and making suggestions to improve your QuickBooks arrangement.

You are instructing your employees on QuickBooks.

Conducting a periodic, comprehensive review of your exchanges as well as a general information and making changes when necessary.

You offer continuous assistance to your business on an "as needed" basis, or for projects which require exceptional skills in bookkeeping and taxes, tax planning and so on.

HOW TO CHOOSE THE RIGHT QUICKBOOKS PLAN

Uncertain of which version of QuickBooks to select? Are you unable to decide whether QuickBooks Online, QuickBooks Desktop or a different version of QuickBooks is the best choice for your company?

With five different things to consider, choosing the most effective QuickBooks software can be a challenge. In addition, the fact it is that QuickBooks isn't always the most sought-after for information on their products!

In this complete QuickBooks Comparison, we'll explain what each program is designed to do, which type of business best suits every version of QuickBooks and the main distinctions between each product. We'll also walk you through the types of questions you should make to determine the best QuickBooks software for your company and choose the most appropriate QuickBooks bookkeeping system with confidence.

Do you not have the chance to read the entire article on correlation? The chart below breaks down the primary differences in QuickBooks Online, QuickBooks Pro, QuickBooks Premier, QuickBooks Enterprise and QuickBooks Self-Employed.

Chapter 5: The Diagram For Quickbooks Products

Quickbooks ONLINE

The program was introduced in 2004. QuickBooks Online is cloud-based bookkeeping program that is utilized by over 2 million users. With robust bookkeeping capabilities with amazing features and mobile apps that are fully-integrated It's not a surprise to learn that this is among of our most popular 5/5-star bookkeeping recommendations.

Ideal to use for...

Small businesses with less more than 25 clients looking for an easy-to-use cloud-based accounting software and robust mobile apps.

Pricing

QuickBooks Online (QBO) offers three estimates that start between $20 and $150 per month. The more extersive the plan is, the more features you can have access to, and the more clients you can allow. The most comprehensive arrangement includes 10 clients (although you are able to get up to 25 members as of 7/31/2019). Payroll expenses range from $35-

$80 per month plus $4/month per representative). It is good news that Intuit has a tendency of conducting a business development. Take a look at our comprehensive QuickBooks Online audit for all the information about pricing.

Features

QuickBooks Online offers several automation and features. It considers every contingency as an invoice and cost-following debtors, creditor liability, managing contacts, task management and the possibilities are endless from there. While there are some issues with routes, QBO is unbelievably simple to use in general.

What distinguishes QuickBooks from other items in the bookkeeping category is the new loaning feature -QuickBooks Capital. QuickBooks Capital. QuickBooks Capital uses the data that is currently available on QuickBooks Online to decide if the small-sized business can qualify to receive the loan.

Some of our other most popular features are:

* Invoice planning

* Class that follows

* Inventory

* Time immediately following

* Print checks

QBO provides over 550 reconciled transactions which is more than the majority of all QuickBooks item.

QuickBooks is often criticized for its poor customer assistance, however QuickBooks Online has is working in recent times to restore its fame by reducing lengthy hold time and improving their assistance area of focus.

If the incorporation of features, ease of use and portability are crucial for the way you work, QuickBooks Online is your best choice. If you're looking to understand the way QuickBooks Online compares to other QuickBooks products, read on.

Quickbooks PRO

The product was launched in 1992. QuickBooks Desktop Pro was the program that has established QuickBooks up for the long haul. The 5/5-star program was private and comes with the most innovative features.

Ideal to use for...

Small to medium-sized businesses with fewer than three clients looking for a solid accounting system or private-introduced programming.

Pricing

There are two pricing options with regard to QuickBooks Desktop Pro. You can choose to purchase an QuickBooks Pro permit for $299.95 or buy a yearly subscription for QuickBooks Pro Plus for $299.95/yr.

If you opt for an QuickBooks Pro permit, it will be in use for a lengthy period of time before Intuit discontinues support for the software. (You are able to, currently however, use the program following the three-year period. However, you will not receive any assistance if something goes wrong.) Phone support costs extra. If you choose QuickBooks Pro Plus, updates as well as telephone support are part of the.

Features

As we have mentioned before, QuickBooks Pro has a amazing array of functions. In terms of bookkeeping is concerned, QuickBooks Pro is one of the most developed solutions available that boasts a diagram-based account and journal sections, bank compromise 130 report options, and some. These incredibly designed features require a lot of learning, but for those who are bookkeepers, have previous experience in bookkeeping, or for the business owner who wants to master their bookkeeping making the time to master QuickBooks Pro can be a great investment.

Most importantly, QuickBooks Pro offers many highlights. But, every component is designed with care. Intuit came up with everything for this one, and even spell-check.

Other of our most popular QuickBooks Desktop Pro features include:

* Invoicing

* The executives are projected.

* Cost of job

Plan and calendar for your day

* Accounts payable

* Budgeting

* Tax assistance

117

QuickBooks Pro offers very nearly 200 integrations this is an outstanding number for a private-owned software. It's not like QuickBooks Online, has QuickBooks Pro yet had poor customer service.

QuickBooks Pro can be an excellent choice for businesses looking for an accounting solution that is robust or private introduction to programming. The requirement to absorb information is a great benefit for those with previous bookkeeping experience or want to have an opportunity to familiarize themselves with the software.

Quickbooks PREMIER

QuickBooks Desktop Premier is the next stage for medium-sized companies seeking a comparable strong accounting system as QuickBooks Pro, yet with greater clients and features that are tailored to the industry (and at a lower price as compared to QuickBooks Enterprise). Working area Premier is a solid private-owned software that has many features and an impressive number of integrations.

Ideal option for...

Small to medium-sized businesses with fewer than five clients that require strong accounting and industry-specific features for bookkeeping.

Pricing

QuickBooks Desktop Premier is all more costly, yet its estimation structure is identical to QuickBooks Pros. There are two options to choose from: either purchase an QuickBooks Premier permit for $499.95 or buy a year-long subscription to QuickBooks Premier Plus for $499.95/yr.

If you opt for QuickBooks Premier, or the QuickBooks Premier permit, telephone support will cost you an additional fee. If you choose QuickBooks Pro Plus, updates and phone support are included. To get the complete scoop read the Complete Guide to QuickBooks Desktop Pricing.

Features

QuickBooks Premier is advanced for solid accounting. Similar to QuickBooks Pro There is an expectation of absorbing data here, however, the software incorporates specific capabilities that Pro requires, such as the ability to market methods, stock assembly and deals that anticipate.

The real thing that separates QuickBooks Premier separated from QuickBooks Pro is the clear features for business. You can choose the basic edition of QuickBooks Premier, or you could choose from five distinct releases: Contractor, Manufacturing and Wholesale, Nonprofit, Professional Services or Retail.

Here are some other options to look forward to with QuickBooks Desktop Premier:

* Industry-explicit reports

* Sales orders

* Print shipping names and print them

QuickBooks Premier offers 190 incorporations and customer support the same as QuickBooks Pro.

Before making a decision on QuickBooks Premier, make sure to keep looking for additional data. It's better not to spend more money if the benefits don't justify the possible benefits.

Quikbooks ENTERPRISE

QuickBooks Desktop Enterprise has a similar amazing accounting capabilities to Pro and Premier However, it allows access to as many as 30 users and a lot more space. With six distinct versions for industry, QuickBooks Enterprise has highly developed features that address the needs of nearly every major company.

The best to use for...

Large organizations with fewer than 30 clients seeking industry-specific accounting and advanced bookkeeping.

Pricing

QuickBooks Desktop Enterprise features three-yearly memberships that include Silver (begins at $1100/year) as well as Gold (begins at $1430/year.) along with Platinum (begins at $1,760).

Costs are controlled by the arrangement you choose and the number of clients you can have. When you purchase QuickBooks Enterprise, you get Intuit Field Management with access for just one client. For the complete scoop on estimation, check out our complete QuickBooks Enterprise survey.

Features

For featuresare concerned, QuickBooks Enterprise is about as similar as you could attain ERP without the need to switch to full-blown business-to-business programming.

Additionally, the robust bookkeeping that you'd expect from QuickBooks Enterprise. In addition to the strong bookkeeping you'd expect from a QuickBooks workspace item. QuickBooks Enterprise offers invoicing costs, cost follow-up, contact the executive team and project management, as well as expenses for work and that's only the beginning.

You can choose the standard version that comes with QuickBooks Desktop Enterprise or choose any of six explicit versions that include options: Construction, Manufacturing and Wholesale, Retail, Nonprofit Professional Services and Accountant.

Other notable attributes are:

1. Lead executive

* Accounts payable

* Inventory

* Business plans

* Loan director

* Tax assistance

Similar to QuickBooks Pro, QuickBooks Enterprise is also compatible with around 200 applications from outside.

QuickBooks support offers the best support to QuickBooks Enterprise clients. The support agents are friendly and responsive There are large quantities of support resources to peruse.

However, QuickBooks Enterprise has its disadvantages. The software is extremely costly and, at the price you're paying for, specific functions such as invoicing, project management time-following, and import are severely restricted. The product is better suited for large companies than for enterprises, which makes the name somewhat confusing.

Quickbooks Self-EMPLOYED

QuickBooks Self-Employed may not be identical to the other QuickBooks Products in that it isn't exactly bookkeeping software. QuickBooks Self-

Employed is a charge-based program designed to aid specialists in handling their accounts, manage evaluated quarterly expenses and figure-based the underlying logic.

Ideal to use for...

Contract workers, freelancers and other self-employed individuals require vital accounting and expense support.

Pricing

There are two options for estimating to use QuickBooks Self-Employed. You can pay for it at $10 per month. To get the full range of featuresthat QuickBooks Self-Employed adds to the table. Alternatively, you can choose to pay $17/month. It will also add an automatic Tax reconciliation with Turbo Tax Reconciliation to your agreement.

Intuit is often operating an expansion of business as such, so be sure to verify any possible limitations prior to purchasing. To learn more details, take a look at our complete QuickBooks Self-Employed Survey.

Features

Similar to QuickBooks Online, QuickBooks Self-Employed is easy to use cloud-based software with powerful mobile apps. The functions are designed specifically for professionals to meet the needs of assessment and reasoning. You are able to easily and without an effort separate your personal and company costs This is great for professionals who don't have separate financial obligations for business.

The software does not only help freelancers navigate the waters of the assessed quarterly fees Additionally, it provides the most essential accounting tools for tracking the cost of pay and expenses.

Here are some of the features that you can expect from QuickBooks Self-Employed

* Invoicing

* Fixed resource devaluation

* Schedule Cs

* Tax agenda

QuickBooks Self-Employed is a limited incorporation However, it's Turbo Tax combination is one of the finest features of the software. When you're ready to record your costs, you can transfer all information from your QuickBooks Self-Employed details and import them into Turbo Tax for easy documentation.

Unfortunately, QuickBooks Self-Employed's customer support is far worse that QuickBooks Pro's. There is no support via phone and the additional help resources are limited. Live chat is available as a feature, which helps you concentrate on the issue you require assistance for.

There's a downside that clients should be aware of: QuickBooks Self-Employed offers government support at a cost, which means you'll have to pay the way your state enforces it.

This being said, QuickBooks Self-Employed is an excellent option for those who are freelancers, temporary employees or other self-employed individuals. If this is the case will not find other QuickBooks product that's customized to meet your specific expenses.

QUALBOOKS ONLINE SELF-EMPLOYED

This variation of QuickBooks is designed for experts. It lets you:

* Track costs and pay

* Keep receipts organized

* Estimated charges

* Invoice customers and confirm installments

* Track miles

* Run essential reports.

Important note with regards to the Self-Employed version When you begin using this type of form it isn't possible to change to a different arrangement. Start using one of the basic software for business below for the possibility to progress to a different arrangement.

Quickbooks ONLINE SIMPLE START:

This version is planned for sole proprietors. It is easy to change to other QuickBooks types as your business expands.

It has everything that an independent-owned form can do and more, as well as the additional features:

* Make sure to send measures

* Deals and deals are tracked and charged.

• Manage temporary employees on 1099

Quickbooks Online Essentials

The next level of online program includes the functions of Self-Employed and Simple Start, in addition to the following:

* Manage your bills

* Time to track

* Include three customers

Quickbooks ONLINE PLUS

The third level of online programming drives the features that accompany it, as well as which are integrated with the older version of the software:

* Include five clients

* Monitor the project's productivity

* Track inventory

The Quickbooks on-line Advanced

The most advanced level access to online content provides the highlights of all previous three releases. In addition, you being able to:

* Pay your bills

* Check out the smart announcement

* Accelerate invoicing

* Design custom consents for clients, and custom fields

* Receive client assistance and prepare

Each online agreement includes the joining of applications, customer assistance with instructional exercises and online resources, as well as additional financing options (cost depending on full-service or self-service in addition to the per-representative cost) and a 30-day trial for free.

Quickbooks DESKTOP PRO Pro PLUS, Mac

The versions for work areas of QuickBooks can be installed via your computer, not being downloaded from the web. The software is not updated except for the Plus version, which is a requirement for an annual subscription fee.

Work area Pro is priced as one-time payment and comes with the following features:

* Track inventory

* Track deals and deal charges

* Send invoices

Manage your bills and keep track of records payable

* Track the cost of pay and expenses.

The Work space Pro Plus requires a yearly expense , and comes with the highlights mentioned above. It also includes unlimited support for clients as well as the reinforcement of information and retrieval as well as access to software updates.

QuickBooks for Mac is like Pro however, despite the fact that it's not as it has a number of features that are upgraded to work on those on the Mac stage (even although QuickBooks website doesn't know what those features are).

Pro and Pro are as well as, to enable the transfer of data to Excel and reconcile to Outlook; Mac empowers fare to Apple Numbers programming, just as it allows you to switch later on the program to Online as well as Windows programming.

Quickbooks DESKTOP PREMIER and PREMIER PLUS

The premier level of QuickBooks work area programming, which demands only one time installment, contains the full functionality of QuickBooks Pro, in addition to the additional features included with it:

* See industry-explicit reports

* Create deals orders

* Track the cost of items and stocks

* Customize reports on stocks

* Five clients can be supported.

Its Premier Plus version, as together with it's Pro Plus adaptation, permits unlimited client support, automated information reinforcement and recovery as well as access to the most current software updates. It is a year-long fee for membership.

Chapter 6: How To Select The Right Version Of Quickbooks For Your Business

If you've read the illustration of every QuickBooks product, then you might at this point be able to determine which version of QuickBooks is the best one for your small-scale company. If not, don't stress. These five questions will help you in narrowing down your query and help you find the answer you're seeking.

Do You Want Cloud-Based Software or Locally-Installed Software?

The most important aspect is whether you require locally or cloud-based software.

Cloud-based software is completely on the cloud (on the internet). Some of the benefits of cloud-based programming are:

* Mobility

Access to a variety of clients across a variety of areas

* SaaS evaluation model based on membership

* Security is handled by the supplier of the product

It is usually incorporated into mobile applications

The software downloaded locally is installed on a single PC on premises. The advantages of installing locally-installed software are:

* No web access needed

* More sophisticated and rich in features

* Potentially becoming more secure (you have to answer for security)

Smaller businesses tend to lean towards cloud-based applications because they are becoming more moderate, easy to use, and is conscious of the mobile lifestyle. However, locally-installed programs can be more secure and provides a level of features that cloud services typically can't connect to.

Selecting the type of program that is best for your particular strategy can make settling on your QuickBooks choice in a much easier manner. If you require cloud-based programming it is available through QuickBooks Online or QuickBooks Self-Employed. If you're looking for locally-installed software, select of QuickBooks Pro, QuickBooks Premier and QuickBooks Enterprise.

Are You a Mac Or Windows User?

QuickBooks Pro, Premier, and Enterprise are designed to work with Windows. In case you're an Mac customer, it's restricted to two options: QuickBooks Online and QuickBooks Enterprise.

What kind of business do You Manage?

The kind of business you operate determines the QuickBooks item is right to be used by you. If you're an expert and want to work from home, QuickBooks Self-Employed is an undisputed choice. If you're operating small-sized businesses You'll need to consider QuickBooks Online and QuickBooks Pro.

The larger companies can consider QuickBooks Premier or QuickBooks Enterprise dependent on the number of customers they require.

How many Users Do You Do You Need?

The amount of clients you'll need will help you determine the best program for your company. Examine this graph to determine what program best suits your company size.

Note: This graph shows the highest number of QuickBooks clients compatible with each QuickBooks version, which could cost you additional.

The amount of accounting Experience Are You Having?

If you don't know about bookkeeping, you'll have to stay clear of QuickBooks Pro, Premier, or Enterprise unless you're willing to take an opportunity to gain knowledge.

QuickBooks Online and QuickBooks Self-Employed are much more straightforward options to figure out when you don't have a lot of knowledge or aren't able to keep changing the book.

However, if you're an accountant or with a great accounting background You might like the complexity of the QuickBooks work space options since they adhere to increasingly traditional accounting procedures.

1. Look for an accountant.

Before you start the process, the first step you must take is talk about moving your money to QuickBooks with a reliable financial expert. In this regard, Intuit offers an online accountant coordination service known as ProAdvisor. But, the majority of accountants are supportive of the administration, so that a local referral could be a substitute.

The reason is a phone conversation or email exchange with the accountant in order to establish and confirm any points of interest regarding your company that QuickBooks requires, such as your business structure, appropriate shows for the following expenses, and your obligations with respect to local or state regulators.

2. Go over the QuickBooks basic concepts.

Learn about the software. Whatever your level of proficiency, proficient with numbers, you should invest your time into the "Beginning" tab of the tutorial exercises that show the method by which QuickBooks is able to handle the invoices you pay and receive and your organization's expenses. QuickBooks categorizes revenue as "Cash In,"" and expenses as "Cash out." The software, at this point determines the flow of these assets throughout your company in a graph known as "Getting About."

3. Create a secure and safe environment.

Security is essential whenever money is at stake in any way, but it is especially important in the case of QuickBooks since your entire financial related activities are within one location. Before you begin entering sensitive financial information, go into"Change Password" in the "Change Password" option in your "Your Account" areaand then create an unique and intricate password. It is also recommended to think about changing your passwords and the ones that QuickBooks stores, as well as your online-based financial IDs on the bank's website, and within QuickBooks each quarter.

4. Input your company's vitals.

As you've learned about the basic QuickBooks features and have you have your passwords in place, go into"Preferences," click on the "Preferences" connect option under"Organization". Click on the "Organization" tab and input your company's financial information as per the basic conversations together with the accountant. In general, the most important things to consider are the structure of your business and revealing structures, tax ID numbers, and a detailed schedule. However, these can vary depending on the company and even the smallest details may be crucial. Make sure you double-check these information by contacting your Financial Advisor through phone or via email.

5. Enter client data.

Then, click on"Client". Now, click on "Client" section and begin adding customer information. While name, address and email are important but the most important element will be that of the "Installment Method" choice. Ask your customers directly to determine whether they prefer to pay via check, money or Visa. Then, you can set the options as needed and, if it is possible make a sample receipt for your clients. Confirm with them that everything is filled in correctly.

6. Include the essential representative and seller details.

Then, click on next, click on the "Vendors" or "Employees" menus. Begin by entering the information for the contact details of those who work on behalf of you and provides services the services you need; however, don't be compelled to input every single detail

QuickBooks demands. Verify each section by generating a report by clicking"Report." Click the "Report" button at the right side part of your screen. There shouldn't be an obligation to choose between alternatives, such as, "Oversee Bills" or "Finance."

7. Begin to follow your cash flow.

The next step is the most difficult of presenting the actual amount your company makes and spends. To do this, go to your "Banking" menu and concentrate on the primary revealing options to track the money you earn and the expenses your company acquires. It is possible to connect with the majority of pertinent budgetary records, like including credit and ledgers from here.

You must ensure that you cut checks using your "Write checks" tab, and track your expenditures and transactions under"Store, "Credit credit card Expense," "Money Expense," and "Store" headings. Test out each of these features to ensure you are able to comprehend the information clearly, and that QuickBooks records the data in a timely manner.

Additionally, you'll need to handle the movements for yourself. It is possible to use"Oversee Users" or the "Oversee the Users" screen located within"Your Account "Your Account" area, to allow clients, but ideally just you as well as your accountant, and to view "Movement" reports, which show the actions that are taking place within the account.

8. Examine expense labels and confirm with the bookkeeper.

The business's data must be separated by class for both expenses and controllers. In this regard you'll need to understand the scattered pieces of information that describe what your business's spending. It is important to understand how you can adhere to "Money Expenses" by hand instead of downloading costs from an account at a bank or Reddit account. This is usually found under the "Downloaded Transactions" segment.

The process of entering cash costs in QuickBooks can be an easy process. Input an amount, assign the seller, and then join an account. Cost information from your bank or Visa records are easily uploaded. Also, it's likely that you should verify with your accountant before you start to ensure that you've named these correctly.

9. Make the first Profit and Loss statement.

After you've examined the costs of your company, this is an ideal time to consider the amount of cash your company earns. Intuit offers a wide array of instruments that reveal information to help you determine your cost marks. For this moment, you should focus specifically on your "Benefit and Loss" report, which is accessible under the "Report" tab. The report on Profit and Loss contains the amount you earned for an entire time period, and then subtracts the cost that you incurred based on the data entered into QuickBooks. Apart from that this report will to give an idea of how much money you'll need near by to pay on your future profit.

Additionally, Intuit offers a "Retain" work-flow that allows you to spot this , and other specific reports every day and then show your accountant these reports.

10. Include features as needed.

Once you have all the nuts and bolts in place Invoicing, deal following cost-checking and deciding the cost or benefit and commitments, you are able to begin adding the features. The next steps could include creating an essential accountancy report, looking into your income announcement and automating the way it is possible to reconcile bank accounts.

QuickBooks provides an application-focused approach to use cutting-edge tools for client relations including the stock, the board and even charging. There are also mobile applications available for Android and iPhone which enable most of the essential QuickBooks online functions.

This includes the first time you've had a customer...

Did you know that you could consolidate your Desktop as well as your online clients with the QuickBooks Online Accounting system? In order to add the work-related customers, it's relatively easy. Look through your files and then browse deals and customers and include the client.

The process of registering an online client is very simple and easy. It is recommended that you insist that the client add your name as an accounting. In my CRM (client relationship to the board program) 17 caps, I have pre-set layouts.

If I receive a message from a client via my contact form, I employ a procedure that allows me to email them a sample email asking for access. The text of the email is as follows: It advises the user to access the account settings, tools to oversee clients, and bookkeeping company. After that, you should include my address for email. It's direct. If a potential customer has issues with this, I've got an instructional video that demonstrates this process. I try to keep the process as simple as possible for the person who could be a future customer.

In addition, an accountant who is a user...

After being invited, I accept the invitation via the email I received from the accountant. Usually, this process is just a couple of clicks. However, as you can see on the following video, this does not fill in the way it was planned. One suggestion is to make sure that you don't have instances of something Intuit displays within the application. When we closed everything and then clicked the welcome button again I was able to go directly to my customer.

Furthermore, here's the official PDF on the most efficient method of transferring the data from QuickBooks Work area to QuickBooks online. Be sure to follow each one of the steps. Be sure to not ignore any. Here are some of the most important things to remember:

These Conversion Tip...

1. Be sure to create the work area records first. Make sure to accommodate the earliest date you can think of. This is a major step in preparing the document before you can process it.

2. I suggest making a handy document of your workspace document and then re-establishing it as your working document. This is the document which you'll change. The flexibility of a document puts the work-related document in an ideal position to make a request. I'm sure it's an added step. But, it's essential to ensure that you are able to have a good, reliable record in case you make the next time.

3. If you change the information over, ensure that you update the document with the most

recent information of significance. In the case of the online document you must make a significant change in order to allow it to be re-accommodated back to the way it was on Desktop.

4. Try a trial parity on both the work areas on the web versions. Verify the data using the date extension all through the detailed basis accrual.

Some thoughts about Wholesale Billing...

This is where we come to a consensus. In the Parkway commercial arrangements Matthew as well as the team take all applications and memberships in their assessment of the client. They will pack everything.

In the case of Artisan Bookkeeping, this was my plan. Due to the constant change in not being able to offer customers who are already customers with discounts and also the half-off discount I decided to shift my outlook to a different location. At present, I've eliminated from the QuickBooks for the Web and payroll subscriptions with full-service in the context of the entire group. The customer is given the chance to pay simply. I encountered the issue of customer pushback during an annual audit I conducted with my clients. Often I would get the message "I paid that much to do your accounting?" The customer would forget the fact that memberships are packaged inside. I make them pay directly.

Don't use my method of estimate (non-packaging) hinder you from using discount charging or packaging. Discount charging offers a unique advantage you can take with your new client even if they're using QuickBooks online at the time they call you. If they call you without accounting software, do not hesitate to bring them in and provide them with the markdown. You could also save the markdown for yourself and include it into your evaluation of the work.

It is important to be settled prior to the event. I am compelled to push to do this as much as I can. Get it from someone who did not do it and was unable to finish the task several times. The work you perform in QuickBooks and their software is a customer's work at the time that the task is completed. If you aren't paid in advance and they do not pay you it's not your fault. take action about it.

This is the most efficient business method. If the client isn't ready to make a payment upfront then suggest that they pay you via a charge card. The customer can typically return their credit card company to contest the charge. If you advise the customer to do this, it can reduce their anxiety about prepaying.

A quick preview of the upcoming week's activities...

We hope these suggestions are helpful as we start to learn more about QuickBooks Online Accountant, and the many benefits that come with QuickBooks Online Accountant. In a week's time, we will examine the preparation of you and your customer and then we'll get to looking at how to be certified by passing the test and all of the incredibly instructive aspects of becoming ProAdvisor. We cannot stress enough how it's so crucial to pass the test and take the Advanced exam to be able to surpass each other up. You will also be registered on the find ProAdvisor site. ProAdvisor website. It will also generate leads. We will be discussing the forms we use for onboarding (they are amazing!) and also applications!

Chapter 7: Basic Steps To Operating Qbooks

Bookkeepers and accountants frequently request what they should to first do to familiarize them with their clients' QuickBooks(r) Online records. Don't be afraid; it's not as hard as it may seem. Here are my top ten steps to settling into QuickBooks Online.

1. Be familiar with the Layout

In contrast to the traditional desktop applications, QuickBooks Online is available across a range of gadgets and frameworks, similar to the software you'd install on your cell tablet or phone. If you're already familiar with desktop applications and cloud-based formats, QuickBooks Online may be a bit difficult to get familiar. Let's go through it piece-by-piece.

Dashboards: Once you click on an organization of a client the page that you land on will display an interactive overview of their invoices, sales expenses, Profit and Loss, as well as Bank Accounts.

Left navigation: On this board, you'll discover the various tabs that you require to use in your clients QuickBooks, grouped by classes. When you select a tab or tab, small subcategories will be displayed at the top. For example, by clicking to the sales tab you'll access these categories: Sales Customers, Invoices, and the Products and Services.

Note Make use of Note: Use the Hamburger symbol (truly it's the real name, not just beyond QuickBooks!) to decrease and increase the left direction to allow you more room to work.

Gear icon: When you tap on the gear icon located in the upper-right corner, you'll have an possibility of accessing your customer's Account, Tools, Settings, Lists and Lists and that's not even the beginning.

Be aware that if a tiny apparatus symbol appears in the upper-right corner of a table, rundown or exchange You'll find options to set the parameters.

Create (+) symbol: All kinds of exercises and exchanges you and your customer are able to perform within QuickBooks Online are in one menu. Select the Make (+) symbol that is located next to the search bar to select the type of exchange you'd like to add.

Bar for searching: This search bar lets you find the exchange in a short time. Bookkeepers may also use it to create an account report or bank register fast.

Enter the report's name or record. By clicking the search box, you will display an ongoing list of exchanges which are added to the book.

Note Take note of Advanced Search in the base right hand corner to refine your search.

Accountant toolkit The menu may be displayed if you're identified as an accountant. There are tools that are not suitable for accountants as well as simple paths to the tools and exchanges that we think you'll use the most.

Drop-down of customers as an accountant, you are able to switch between clients or jump into your classes by clicking on the drop-down menu for customers. If you have a large listing of clients, quickly switch to the customer you're looking for by typing your company's name within the Search for a Customer field.

2. Configure the Settings

Under the Gear Menu you'll find the Account and Settings. This is where you and your customers will be able to modify the settings of their QuickBooks Online to fit the requirements of their business most effectively.

When you are in within the Account and Settings section I suggest everyone who uses accountants to familiarize themselves with the tab for advanced. There are options such as closing books, close the Books (where there is the option to choose an expiration date as well as a password) and also enable Account Numbers.

Be aware that the Billing and Subscription tab will be displayed in the event that your customer pays to join. If you're using Wholesale Billing and Subscriptions, you'll have to deal the customer's charges as well as membership via your QuickBooks Online Accountant.

3. Install an acccunt Chart of Accounts

A stunning Chart of Accounts is critical to a solid reporting. You car access your chart via the rigging symbols menu and in the tab for Accounting on the left or in your Toolbox for Accountants. It is possible to set up your Chart of Accounts physically or by importing a recent list of accounts from Excel. If you've made a change to the QuickBooks Desktop of a client then your Chart of Accounts changes over too.

Use the pencil symbol on the upper right hand corner to assign or change account numbers/names in a set, instead of changing each one individually.

The drop-down menus beneath the Action section to the far right hand side offer the option to change accounts only erase or erase information or mark them as inactive.

4. Associate Bank and Credit Card Accounts

If you're not yet collaborate with your clients to connect them with their financial institutions, which will allow you to reduce time and speed of information flow. This can be done through the Banking tab on the left navigation.

If the records are connected with QuickBooks, you can review the records, make an order, and accept transactions from the bank into QuickBooks. QuickBooks Online has worked in auto-categorization, which gains your account after a certain period of time. Additionally, you have the option to make a match with the transactions within the account.

Switch into on the Bank Rules tab along the top to alter the way QuickBooks Online classifies exchanges. This is especially helpful for those who aren't sure what to do to sort exchanges or who have a large volume of exchanges that are comparable. Take a look at my ongoing arrangement of bank feeds.

5. Create Transactions that Recurre

If your client is using QuickBooks Online Essentials or Plus there is a possibility to set up a variety of transactions that run on a regular basis. They can be set up by clicking the gear-icon menu. Automating transactions can help save timing and improves precision, especially when combined in conjunction with the feed from banks.

You can set up transactions to be automated and set up updates and create templates that are not scheduled.

6. Create a My Custom Reports List

Visit The Reports tab to access the report list that will be remembered to your customer's account. It is possible to design the majority of reports using QuickBooks Online to meet best the needs of your customers and you as well as other reports that you can customize for future use. Once you've completed the My Custom Reports list from the toolbox of accountants.

We display a selection of often as possible alternatives on the top of every report, to make it easier to quickly customize such as choosing the period for your report or changing between the basis of gathering and money. Always click Run report to update your report.

Click Customize on the upper right hand corner to access the options to customize the report. The customization options will vary depending on the report you're running.

Once your preferences have been in place, simply save the changes to add it to the My Custom Reports list. If you save, you'll be given the option of giving your customized report a title, include it to a group when you want, and then decide to make it available to all customers or only your company.

Within the My Custom Reports show, you can run your reports, convert to PDF, alter the settings for sharing, and look at reports that others have shared with you.

You can also plan one report or a set of reports to send out with a scheduled schedule.

7. View Windows Side-by-Side

Through program tabs, users are able to open various windows within QuickBooks Online simultaneously. This allows you to cross-reference, analyze, or do a variety of tasks without closing the page you're working on.

Accountants can also take advantage of a straightforward option under the accountant toolkit known as New Window, which will duplicate your current page into another tab.

In many applications you can also click a tab with the right mouse button and then left-click Duplicate.

You can use the identical number of tabs needed and drag them across multiple screens.

8. Review the Audit Log

Under the gear-icon symbol for the apparatus menu, you'll find an Audit Log. This log keeps track of the increases and modifications made to the information of the organization as well as other activities. It also tracks who logs into the company.

The review log isn't restricted or erased. You can organize it through date, client as well as movement. You can examine changes over certain period of time.

Notice: If your client reviews the log, we do not display any information about your client, but only the name of the company.

9. Explore the Toolsbox for the Accountant Toolbox

According to the article in the article, accountants are able to locate instruments that are preferred by accountants, but only as alternative methods to exchange and tools which we expect you to use the most.

Here are some tools for accountants that you must be aware of:

Trial Balance allows you to review and alter the books to prepare for the government form without the need to bounce between multiple applications. You can also create maps of accounts and create, view and record a government form using Intuit(r) ProConnect(tm) Tax Online.

Rename Transactions can be used for group changes to the group as well as keep track of various kinds of exchanges.

Reports Tools lets you choose the default date and time range for various reports related to money and other accounting devices.

Bookkeepers also have the option to examine a diary entry for alterations and then fix reconciliation.

10. Be certified (and see your company grow!)

There's no better way to follow your QuickBooks Online training than using our no-cost ProAdvisor(r) program within QuickBooks Online Accountant.

You can take the QuickBooks Online Certification course in the Training tab to increase your knowledge (and get CPE!). When you've passed the certification exam you'll be able to enjoy the benefit of unlimited U.S. -based proAdvisor phone support as well as the option to include your information in the Find-A ProAdvisor online index that makes it easier for prospective customers to locate your profile.

QuickBooks Online Advanced Payroll - Beginning.

Utilizing standard QuickBooks Online Payroll? Click on Turn On and configure the payroll.

Follow this guideline to finish your finance agreement quickly and accurately

Documents required

The information below can make the process of arranging easier:

1. Your payroll account is registered with your Canada Revenue Agency (CRA) It has crucial details about your company, such as your legal name, address of work and CRA financial account numbers. Also, you'll need the confirmation letter from the CRA that outlines your remittance frequency.

2. A check drawn from your company's financial account or another document which contains all financial details needed to conclude your bank agreement.

3. Documents you've received from commonplace expense organisations or worksheets, such as your Workers' pay account details , or other relevant commonplace

assessments like those for the Employer Health Tax in Ontario

4. Your government's workers' and standard TD1 forms, with all the important personal details, like complete names, date of birth as well as Social Insurance Number (SIN) completed.

5. A copy of the voided check from each of your contractors or employees to establish the direct store

If you're trading payroll providers, you need to create a record of all compensation for employees, and any expenses paid, as well as the amounts of any business costs. These data must be entered in QuickBooks Online Advanced Payroll as part of the annual reporting obligations.

Sign up to receive QuickBooks Online Advanced Payroll

1. Open your QuickBooks Online record.

2. Go to the Employees tab.

3. Choose Payroll and set it up.

4. Select the features available to you in order to view the item-to-item correlation between our two financial contributions.

5. Utilize the cost calculator on one side of the outline to determine your possible expenses in QuickBooks Online Advanced Payroll.

6. You can try a free trial for 30 days in the Advanced Payroll managed by wage point section.

7. Connect and select Agree.

Set-up

After you've signed up the site, you'll be presented with the Setup finance screen, which has five segments that complete the.

* Click Add to input the information in each segment.

* You are also able to edit an element prior to presenting the data. Find out more information on the required data for each section.

Enter your organization data

Please provide us with some information about your company. We'll use this information on your tax returns for payroll.

1. Legal company name (The company name that you apply on government forms and official documents),

2. The location of the company, Email (We'll send you information about our finances and financial reports)

3. Telephone number (utilized to obtain tax documents)

4. You may also enter the Promo Code if one was offered.

5. After that, click done.

Enter your payroll tax details

We offer all-expense monthly installments for the service to your benefit. If you'd prefer to make the installments yourself You can disable this option. Remittances for quarterly payments are not being honored currently. If you're not sure please get in touch with the CRA for further information.

Number of CRA account

* Payroll account number: Your 9-digit business number + RP + your 4-digit account number. (Like this: 123456789 RP0001)

* You'll use the payroll account number for identifying you before the CRA on forms for finance or when you send charges.

* Quebec finance account number: You're 10-digit Quebec Enterprise Number (NEQ) + RS + your 4-digit account number. (Like this: 1234567890 RS0001)

* You'll use the Quebec Finance number, which you can use to differentiate you against Revenue Quebec on payroll forms or when you make payments for charges for payroll.

Note: Make sure the numbers are correct so that you do not miss installments.

Remittance frequency

The frequency of your remittances tells us the frequency at which you pay the financial assessments to CRA and Revenue Quebec. This is in addition to the fees you incur and the responsibilities you get from your workers' checks. If you find that the CRA and Revenue Quebec hasn't revealed to you when to send your tax returns, choose the month-to-month option. They'll inform you of when you should begin sending your taxes more frequently and you'll be able to alter your frequency in your finance settings at any time.

Be aware that if you opt for this option it will be deducted from the balance of your financial records when you do payroll. They will be placed in trust and then remitted to you in accordance with the remittance frequency that you chose at the time of setting up. For more information about Remittance frequencies, if not too difficult you can visit Canada.ca. QuickBooks Online Advanced Payroll naturally determines the interval for payroll and pay dates following your first financing within the framework.

Workers receive'remuneration

It covers the loss of income, Social Insurance and rehabilitation services for those who suffer injuries while at work. It also protects your company from claims made by injured workers. If you employ employees or representatives then you'll likely have to contribute to the workers' compensation. In this case, you should provide your rates so that we can calculate and transfer your obligation. In the present, you be required to report any an insurable amount to the laborers compensation board. If you're unsure of the exact WCB rate is, are interested in looking up this website from the Canadian Center for Occupational Health and Safety for more details.

To add an WCB rate, click the rate you want to include and then choose your:

Province

* Account Number (The number that your regular Workers pay board provided you with when you signed up)

*Rate (Rate is provided by the commonplace experts' compensation board

* When completed, choose done.

Be aware that you may see an opportunity to obtain Revenue Quebec information if your central command is located in Quebec or you have employees who work in Quebec.

Include banking data

Important: Please allow for two to four business days after you've completed each of the three elements of ledger approval to allow your record to be verified and ready to process payroll.

* Micro-deposit verification

* Transfer of ID/Cheque

* Check for Yodlee

Note Attention: Direct store, workers Pay and Source conclusions are removed as one amount, and appear in your bank's explanation that it is the Intuit Trust Payment. Your invoices can be viewed within the report segment.

1. Include the name and email of the authorized official of the bank marking for the bank account that is being used. The bank marking official who is approved or signatory who has been approved should be added as an Company administrator, with access for accounts. QBO account.

2. Choose your Bank name from the drop-down list and then enter your Transit number as well as your Account number.

3. Select the type of account you want to use (Business or Personal)

4. The official who is the authorized marker for the business must be in agreement to the conditions of the Pre-approved agreement on the charge plan

5. Upload the required reports annul the Cheque for the balance of funds and issued the personal ID of the marking official who has been approved.

6. Log into your online banking account to complete the step of confirmation

7. Once you're done, choose done

8. You will not be able to finance until you've completed the micro-deposit as well as Yodlee check. (2-4 business days from the time of your arrangement)

A) Verify your balance in the financial account for the test sum.

B) Choose the Gear symbol that is at the top. At the point you can change your Payroll settings.

C) Select the bank account you want to use

d) Enter the amount for the exchange test into the field that is provided

e) Select Complete approval

f) Select Verify Account

G) Select to start on the screen that opens up

H) Choose your bank's foundation from the list of options

I) Input your online bank account details. Web-based financial certificates cannot be relegated or discarded.

J) Choose the ledger you created in Advanced Payroll

K) Select Confirm

9. Risk and Compliance Risk and Compliance group audits the data to accommodate your new balance in the financial system (2 to 4 business days following the time when setup is completed).

10. Once the catch is approved once it is approved, after approval, the Run Finance Catch will then be made operational

Payroll must be processed three days prior to the date of your compensation. This means that the essential financials should also be available in your balance of funds three days prior to the day of your compensation.

Change the payroll settings to your payroll

This segment includes three tabs: Setup Pay gatherings, Income and deductions.

1. Pay timetable: Add workers or temporary staff to groups that pay. To help you get started at starting out, we've included a few default groups.

a. Select Pay Plan Add

b. You can choose from five frequencies that include: Weekly, Bi-week following week, semi-month to month and monthly. You can also choose to browse quarterly

C. Once you have selected a Frequency You can name it using the fields that is provided

D. Select Done when you are done

2. Income sort - Add in the types of money you pay to temporary or employed workers. We've started with the most common ones. You may also request a different kind of salary if you do not know what you're looking for.

Include an income

a. Select the type Add Income

b. Select the type of income from the drop-down list. You can change the way this list appears on pay stubs . Simply type in an income name in the field provided.

If you check the bottom of your screen the pay type, you'll see if the pay type is Taxable Payable, Pensionable, or Insurable. These are CRA normal options, and you will not be able to change these settings.

To request a custom income type:

a. Select Request a custom salary

b. Enter the name of the Income type you want to use

C. You can also decide the appropriate charges (CPP/QPP EI, CPP/QPP Tax provincial tax, health charges and due)

d. You may also choose which one (14/A 40/L, 14/A, or other) this amount will appear on the form T4/Releve.

E. Note any additional notes and then choose to send when you are done

F. You will receive an email that will let you know if your request was included in the list.

Note: You can provide an ongoing pay (reward or additional time, event and an excursion) for temporary workers as well as permanent workers.

3. Benefits/Deductions - These include things like health benefits or RRSP commitments you can deduct from temporary workers Compensation. It is also possible to request another reasoning type if you do not recognize the one you're looking for.

To add another factual result:

a. Select Add derivation/advantage

b. Select the Deduction/advantage type from the drop-down list. You can alter how it appears on your pay stubs, by entering the name of the Deduction or Advantage in the box provided.

C. If you go to the bottom to see what you can do, you'll find out if the pay type is Taxable or Pensionable. Insurable. This is CRA standard configurations, and you will not be able to change these settings.

To request a customized reasoning/advantage type:

a. Select Request custom conclusion. You'll receive an e-book box that will help you understand your deduction demand.

b. Select Send after the process is complete.

C. You'll receive an email confirming that your request was included on the list.

d. When you are finished by this section, click Save or Return to the list of tasks.

Include contractors and employees

In this section it is possible to include workers and temporary employees that you paid prior to this tax year.

1. If you click the Add button for this section and you'll be able to see the window that lets you to add a person to your payroll

2. Input their Name and Last Name.

3. Decide if they're an employee or a contractor.

4. Select Yes or No when you're asked, "Have you paid this person in 2017 by yourself or through Payroll services for accountants?"

5. Select Add when you are done

6. You'll be able to see a couple of tabs on the screen:

* Profile Name, Social Insurance number (SIN) and date of birth (DOB) Date of hire address, email Phone

* Employment Compensation rate, Hours from every week, pay gathering Departments, Locations, Job titles Workers' Compensation rates, the vacation plan

* Taxes Federal TD-1 sum Retentions additional, work Area Provincial TD1, Income Tax/CPP/EI Exempt

* Direct Deposit Add banking information for Direct Deposit by Employee deposit priority and Bank's Transit Number along with the account number. (This is used to pay for service charges as well as direct store)

* Income: Types of income such as Amount, Frequency and hours related

* Deductions: Type of Deduction and amount, frequency, employee commitment, company contribution

Important: Make sure to record every representatives' YTD pay history prior to making payroll.

1. Fill in the information required for each tab, then click Save.

AFFECT YOUR CHART OF ACCOUNTS

We have created a few standard accounts for you to begin your journey. It is recommended to select which one you want to use for your Bank account. You are able to look into each of the areas in order to ensure that everything is in the correct place within Your QuickBooks Online records.

2. Select your bank account starting in the drop-down list. This is where you'll see the payroll fees which are deducted from the bank. You can also create a second record using this screen.

3. Choose the Advanced drop-down menu to view the most popular accounts.

4. You can select the highest-level record to view all sub-accounts that are part of it.

5. You are able to alter any records you want and select completed after you are done.

Updates:

• If the focus on business charges set within QuickBooks Online, you will benefit from the Sales Charge on processing costs.

* If the business cost does not have a focus the sales charge, you'll need to make use of Sales cost costs.

* If you're unsure of what you should do to track credit or charges, you should talk to an accountant.

1. To alter the agreement has been made:

2. Choose from the Gear symbol.

3. Select Payroll settings.

4. Click on tabs Chart of the records tab.

There are two diary entries for each pay period.

Journal Entry 1

* Syncs with your QBO account the day pay is made

* debits the clearing records and credits the balance in the financial accounts.

Journal Entry 2

* The synchronization process will be synchronized to your QBO account at the time of your compensation date

* Credits to the clearing account charge fees and obligations.

CREATE and edit, as well as manage BUDGETS

QuickBooks Online Plus has an simple-to-use budgeting feature. Budgeting helps you in making plans to stay in the upper echelon of your costs and revenue. Once you've set up one use your Budget versus Actuals report to assist you in making informed decisions for your company.

The year's money-related year's first month.

The spending starts with the initial month in your money-related year, therefore it's an excellent idea to ensure your Financial Year setting is exact.

To confirm or alter the year of financial reporting:

1. Select the Settings .

2. Choose Account and then Settings.

3. Select Advanced.

4. In the Accounting section Check that the setting in the initial month of the field for the financial year is correct, or click the pencil icon to alter the setting.

5. Choose Save.

6. Select Done.

If you've verified that the year in which you are based on money is correct, the next step is to review the data you plan to gather to determine your budget and ensure that it's accurate.

Check out the historical amounts

It is possible to create your budget for spending based on information or from the present money related year or previous years' amounts. If you are planning to use data from the past it is a good idea to conduct an Profit or Loss Detail report to ensure the exchanges were properly assigned prior to.

In essence the report will display the exchanges that occurred during the current year's monetary year up to date however, you are able to alter your report in order to reveal prior year's value of the year's currency.

1. Re-do this report: Profit and loss Detail report:

2. Select Reports.

3. Open The Profit as well as loss Detail report.

Select the Last Financial Year (or Last Year in January if it is the first month in your financial calendar) in the Report time-frame drop-down menu to make use of the previous year's data. To use information that is from the current fiscal year, accept the default setting for This Year-to-date.

4. Select Run report.

The report contains information from the year that you have a financial connection to have indicated. This report can be used to verify that the transactions you wish to combine your financial limit on were correctly allocated.

Once you've confirmed that you have the correct information to use in your budget, the next step is to create it.

Create your budget

It is now possible to determine your budget limit. The Budgets highlight will help you create the first budget.

To establish an budget:

1. Select the Settings .

2. Under Tools, choose Budgeting.

3. Select the option to add a spending plan.

4. Input a name for your spending in the field Name.

5. In the Financial Year drop-down list, choose the year that is money-related to budget.

6. Utilize the options from the Interval drop-down menu to indicate if the budget is monthly quarterly, annually, or Quarterly.

7. (Optional) (Optional) From the Pre-fill drop-down list Indicate whether to add information from the current or a prior calendar year in the budget and decide which year that you want to use.

8. (Optional) (Optional) From the drop-down menu for Subdivide by Decide if you wish to split the budget according to Class or Customer or by the location. At that point you should

indicate which class, customer or location you want to include in the budget.

If you do not find any options for Class or Location These settings aren't switched on. You can enable them by clicking on the Categories section in the Advanced tab Account and Settings, accessible via the Gear icon in the toolbar.

9. Select Next.

10. If you didn't use the Pre-fill feature input the data into the table. Be aware that QuickBooks Online acknowledges decimals and does not update to the closest dollar. It is possible to change the amount anytime. In the event that you aren't able to see all of your subaccounts and records Select the Gear symbol above the Total section and verify that the Hide clear columns option is selected.

11. Choose Save or Save then then close.

The budget you have set is saved and is recorded in the window for Budgets.

Budgetary reports

The following reports of the budget you created:

A Budget Summary: A summary of budgeted amount for a budget.

The Budget against the Actuals A summary of budgeted amounts and actual amounts , and their variations and rates of fluctuation.

To access the report, email, print or print these reports:

1. Select the Settings .

2. Under Tools, choose Budgeting.

3. Find the monetary allowance you want to view, send an email print, or export.

4. In the drop-down menu in the Action column, choose Run Budget Overview report or Run Budget versus Actuals report.

5. When you are on the Report page, choose from the Report page, click on either Email and Print icon. In the Print email, print or print as PDF dialog choose whether to print or send out an Email along with the report on the budget or Print copies of the budget limit. You can also save the report in PDF form this dialog.

6. (Optional) Choose the Export icon, then select Export in Excel, or Export as PDF in the

drop-down list, to distribute the data within your budget. To view the report, print it, email it, or print an alternative report, choose another option from the Budget drop-down menu.

Edit, copy or remove the existing budget

When you prepare a new budget, your previous spending reports will not be rewritten or altered.

To alter the plan you have then you need to change each line individually.

To edit a current spending plan:

1. Select the Settings .

2. Under Tools, choose Budgeting.

3. Edit the budget.

4. From the drop-down menu for the Action column menu, choose Edit.

5. Make changes to the budget name or budget amount for each of the accounts that are comparing If necessary.

6. (Optional) To subdivide budgets, choose one of the choices from the drop-down menu of

Show rows field to modify the criteria that the budget is subdivided according to.

7. (Optional) (Optional) Click (Optional) the Gear icon above the Total segment, and select Month (Optional) Select Quarter, Year, or Month under View by to alter the budget interval.

8. Choose Save or Save and close.

9. The budget is adjusted to reflect the latest information or your settings.

To duplicate the budget

Copying your current budget lets you make a second spending plan using your budget figures. This is particularly useful if you want to make use of the information from your budget for a prior budget year to come up with a new one.

1. Select the Settings .

2. Under Tools, choose Budgeting.

3. Copy the budget.

4. From the drop-down menu for the Action column menu, choose Copy from the drop-down menu.

5. In the Copy Budget screen, type in the name of your new expenditure and the financial year.

6. Select the Create Budget option.

7. Change the budget amount to be the most fundamental.

8. Choose Save or Save after which you then close.

It is then copied using the name year, as well as the spending amounts you have determined.

To delete a current spending plan:

You may delete your budget from the past, however you should exercise this.

If a budget is deleted, it cannot be restored. The activity log is an account of the budget that was deleted. But, it doesn't provide any insight into the deletion.

1. Select the Settings .

2. Under Tools, choose Budgeting.

3. From the drop-down Action column menu, choose Delete.

The budget has been completely erased and cannot be restored.

Financial Reports and Features for Reporting

Reports appear within Reports tabs appear in the Reports Tab Dashboard list (Reports Center) You can search for something specific by using the search feature on the right. There is a huge amount of reports available. The majority of them will follow this titling method:

Some report on very specific utilization instances, providing you with a variety of possibilities. There are some basic reports that which you'll require to run on each day or week following week's premise, such as,

* Balance Sheet (which follows it's Balance Sheet Equation) is a record of the liabilities, assets and the value of your company - the amount is "own" as well as what you "owe" within a certain period of time.